Sacrifice And Service

A World War II Paratrooper's Story

By Linda Dudik, Ph.D.

Printed in the United States of America

http://www.wwiiexperience.com

PO Box 126
San Marcos, CA 92079

You know them, the men and women of the World War II Generation. Depending on your age, they are your husband, your wife, your parents, your grandparents, or perhaps your great-grandparents. Together, members of that generation lived through two momentous events--the Depression and then the greatest war of the 20ᵗʰ century. Their sense of community sustained them throughout both of those ordeals.

We dedicate this book to them, especially to Dick Field, a man from a small town in New York called Liberty. During a childhood bout with polio, his mother read to him from *The Little Engine That Could*. It became a favorite book of Dick's when he was young. One could argue that its famous refrain--"I think I can, I think I can"--became a mantra for his generation. In the island campaigns of the Pacific, on the battlefields of Europe, and on the Home Front within the States, Americans believed that the Allies would eventually triumph in the war. They continued to trust in that even as casualties mounted year after year. Sacrifice and service appear as themes throughout the personal histories of the men, women, and even children of the World War II Generation. Dick Field's is one such story.

Contents

Contents

The 551st Parachute Infantry Battalion's patch dates from its 1943 combat tour in Panama. The palm tree and the machete reflect the tropics. The lightning bolt refers to the speed at which troopers deployed. The Spanish phrase at the bottom translates "land and attack."

An acronym for the 551st originally used by the unit's commander also originated in Central America. Lt. Colonel Wood Joerg referred to his men as "GOYA birds," or simply "GOYAs." In polite company, it is translated as "Great Outstanding Young Americans." Among members of the 551st, it meant "Get Off Your Ass."

Chapter 1

Early Years in a Small Town and a Big City
"The best of two worlds"

Raised in New York State during the 1920s and 1930s, Dick Field experienced its small-town life as well as its more cosmopolitan side. He was born in Liberty, which had a population of some three thousand people during Dick's childhood. His first eight or nine years were spent in this rural town. By the time he reached his tenth birthday, however, his father had moved to New York City. Only London surpassed its metropolitan population of seven and a half million people. Within New York City, the East Bronx became Dick's home. For about eight years, he spent the school year there with his father and the summer in Liberty with his mother. Dick easily moved back and forth between those two worlds, enjoying the benefits each offered. Just months after the United States entered World War II, Dick left high school. He eventually entered the Army, serving in an elite unit, the 551st Parachute Infantry Battalion. By war's end, Dick wore the campaign ribbons of a decorated paratrooper. He drew on lessons learned in both of those New York worlds--Liberty and the East Bronx--during his wartime service.[1]

Both of Dick's parents came from Sullivan County, located in the southeastern part of New York State. In the early 20th century, tourism associated with the nearby Catskill Mountains became the county's primary industry. Railroads carried visitors, especially in the hot summer months, to the lakes and rivers that marked the landscape.[2] Dick's father and mother came from small communities in the county. Arch ("Archie") Lester Field's hometown was Neversink, while Esther Marie Dexheimer (also known as "Dolly") grew up in Beaver Brook. Archie was born in 1890 and Esther about that same year.[3] Dick's mother appears to have been an independent woman in more than one way. Though small in stature, Esther was strong-willed. She might have learned at an early age to assert herself, a circumstance dictated perhaps by the fact that she was one of thirteen children from a farming family. While some youngsters could be lost in such a brood, Esther's life later indicates that she knew how to make her own way in the world at an early age. At a time when most women in rural areas married young, Esther was still single at age twenty-five. And she had a career.

Dick's mother must have enjoyed learning because she became a teacher in at least two Sullivan County one-room schoolhouses before she married. Altogether, Esther taught for eight years, starting at age seventeen. One school that hired her was in Beechwoods. There in 1913, Esther oversaw the printing of a small booklet entitled "Public School Souvenir." She kept the publication her entire life. The focus point of the cover is a photograph of Esther. One page in it reads, "In memory of days spent in the schoolroom, this token is presented with the compliments of your teacher." A list of school administrators for "Public School No.7" appears on the main page on the inside of the booklet. The teacher's name, "Esther M. Dexheimer," is prominently spotlighted on that same page, with all letters capitalized. Those large letters, and the fact that Esther kept the booklet her whole life, attest to the pride she must have felt as a teacher. The publication was a gift from Esther to her students. Fittingly, it is the list of student names that dominates the main page. Sixteen names of boys are followed by nineteen girls' names.[4] Thirty-five students made Esther's class a large one. In 1915, two years after the class graduated from Beechwoods, almost half of New York's eight thousand one-room schools had ten students or less.[5] A small salary would have accompanied Esther's heavy teaching load. In the mid-17th century, the first schoolteacher Dutch officials appointed on Manhattan Island, then known as New

Amsterdam, received such a paltry sum that he had to take in laundry to survive.[6] Districts historically underpaid teachers, especially once women came to dominate the field in the early 19th century. In spite of the low pay, Dick believes his mother found teaching to be "rewarding." She shared with her children stories from those years. Esther described the potbelly stove that kept the schoolroom warm in the winter months. (She would have risen at an early hour to stoke the fire.) Dick's mother also explained how she confronted farmers who kept their children home from school. Esther did not discount the importance of a formal education, a value that would factor into

Esther and her students

decisions she later made about the schooling of her sons.

What signaled the end of her teaching career was her marriage to Archie Field. Esther visited relatives in Liberty, where she probably met Archie who had moved to that town from Neversink. Esther kept an announcement of their marriage that appeared in the *Sullivan County Democrat* newspaper. The ceremony took place in the Beaver Brook home of Esther's mother on a Saturday afternoon, November 6, 1915. After a honeymoon trip in Archie's Rambler to Poughkeepsie, New York, the newlyweds settled in at 19 Academy Street in Liberty. Society in the early 20th century frowned upon a married woman working outside of the home. As a matter of policy, school districts did not employ married women. The couple lived on the income Archie earned as an automobile mechanic. America's April 1917 entry into World War I interrupted their lives, however. In compliance with a Congressional draft law, Archie registered on June 5, 1917. He described himself as a blue-eyed, red-haired man of medium build. With his mechanical skills, the Army sent Archie overseas to France where he worked on planes. Since the military used aircraft primarily for communication purposes in World War I, such as reporting on movements of enemy troops, airplane crews served in the Signal Corps. In his home today, Dick displays his father's dog tags. They carry Archie's formal designation as a MMSC, Master Mechanic, Signal Corps. Archie, though, did not remain in France until the war ended. Esther became seriously ill and he returned home early. He was discharged in June 1919. By the 1920s, Archie established his own garage in Liberty where he worked on automobiles; his repair shop stood behind the house.

After World War I ended, the Field home at 147 Mill Street began to be filled with children. Esther gave birth to five babies in the house--Charles ("Allen") born in 1920, Arch Jr. in 1922, Dick in 1924, Jeanette who arrived in the late 1920s, and Carol who was born in 1931. Unfortunately, Jeanette died very young, probably in her first year. The three Field boys did temporarily have a "sister" before Carol was born. By 1930 their cousin Mary Dexheimer, the daughter of Esther's brother Jess, had moved in with them. Mary's parents lived on a farm in Beaver Brook, adjacent to Esther's childhood home. After Mary's mother died, Jess asked Esther to take his daughter in. Mary remained in the Field household until Jess remarried, at which time Mary returned to her Beaver Brook home.[7] In the America of today, members of extended families still help each other out, but not to the same degree as in Dick's childhood years. A more modern transportation system, with highways and passenger air travel, appeared after World War II, as did career opportunities that multiplied in those same years. Such developments facilitated the movements of people. Today, cousins might know of each other, but large numbers do not know each other like the Field boys knew Mary Dexheimer. As with her cousins, she grew up in a small town that might seem quaint to many Americans today.

Dick Field speaks fondly of his childhood years in Liberty. He recalls the community as, "a fun place to grow up in." Certainly it appeared as an idyllic, small town where the Presbyterian church steeple with its white spire reached toward the sky. On holidays such as the 4th of July, families gathered at the high school's athletic field to listen to local, school bands. When Dick was growing up in

Liberty, a large hospital stood in the town, dedicated to the treatment of tuberculosis patients. People traveled great distances to be cared for there. But what drew visitors to Liberty, situated about one hundred miles from the Catskill Mountains, was its status as "a year-round resort." [8] Several streams flowed in and out of the town; Dick recalls one that went right down the middle of Liberty. Yet none reached the

Dick on left, Arch Jr. on right

size of a river. Boys and girls could enjoy wading in the shallow waters of the streams or throwing stones across them, while parents never worried about their children being swept away. One small stream ran near the Field home, only about half a mile away. After it was dammed up, the children had a swimming hole. At an elevation of about 1,500 feet, hills also dotted the landscape of Liberty.[9] The geography made the town a natural playground for its youth. Summer meant endless outdoor adventures, real and imagined. The snow brought by winter meant sled rides down hillsides. Liberty also hosted winter carnivals.[10]

Dick's outdoor adventures could have been seriously curtailed when he suffered a bout with polio. He was around five years old at the time, but the paralysis weakened only his face muscles. Dick recalls Esther constantly putting wet towels on his face. He also remembers his mother reading to him from a collection of children's books that the Field family still owns. Dick particularly favored one story that became a classic, *The Little Engine That Could*. The tale stressed the rewards of perseverance as a small train succeeded in a task that larger, more powerful engines refused to take on. The "little engine" kept repeating to herself, "I think I can, I think I can" as she pulled a long train over a high mountain. It took Dick months to recover from the polio. His favorite story during that time may have given him a role model he drew on then and perhaps at other times in his adult life.

If Dick was five when he was struck by polio, it was about that time when the Stock Market "crashed" as stock prices plummeted. A year later, the United States clearly was in an economic downturn that became known as the Great Depression. Dick believes that people in small towns felt it less harshly than those in urban areas. He points out that residents of Sullivan County ate their own chickens, vegetables from family gardens, and wild berries in the fields that surrounded Liberty. Tables were thus not completely devoid of food. Esther also canned, but Dick reminds the listener that there were still items that had to be purchased, such as sugar. He concisely sums up a youth spent growing up in the Depression decade of the 1930s with the phrase, "times were tough." Esther took in what Dick's generation calls "roomers," or boarders. The Field home on Mill Street had four bedrooms. If a roomer showed up, Esther often gave the man one of the rooms belonging to her sons. Dick and his brothers vacated their room. Most of the time, the brothers slept in the attic. As Dick plainly states, "We were poor, but so was everyone else." Although he mentioned only the local food supply as mitigating the effects of the Depression, Dick would also acknowledge the sense of community that existed in small towns. That, too, would have buffered people when the economy declined as neighbor helped neighbor.

Not all Liberty residents were caring people, though. One of Dick's early memories is a hurtful one. When he was six or seven years old, Esther got her youngest son a pair of used shoes. Dick showed up in Liberty's central school with sneakers that were clearly too large for his feet. The gym teacher, Coach Ross, ridiculed him. Dick wore hand-me-down shoes because the Fields were "dirt poor," to use Dick's words. Yet even with a tight family budget, Esther did something for her sons that is mystifying when one understands that she was "a frugal" woman, as her youngest son describes her. When Dick was about seven or eight, his mother bought a baby grand piano. She herself did not know how to play it, nor did Archie. But Esther wanted her sons to learn how to do so. Why this proved important to Esther is something one can only guess at. Certainly, during the 1920s and 1930s, introducing one's children to music meant introducing them to one of the refinements in life. Middle-class families throughout the country gave their children piano lessons for that purpose. A former teacher, Esther believed in a broad education. Aside from the cost of the baby grand itself, somehow Esther also found the money for piano lessons. She may have bartered to pay for them, but Dick is sure his mother paid cash for the piano. Esther arranged for lessons from Eva Engle, a woman who played the church organ. Of the three boys, only Dick took to the piano. He learned how to play after six months or so of lessons. Today that piano stands in Dick's living room.

Dick's life in Liberty took an unusual turn when his parents separated. He was nine or ten, around the same time when golfers at the Grossinger Golf Club in nearby Ferndale hired him as a caddy. One earlier summer Dick had sold newspapers at the local hotels, but the caddying job was the first one that paid him what Dick calls "decent money." A job naturally leads to feelings of independence. His parents' decision to live apart would have increased that feeling even more as Dick learned to move back and forth between two homes. Dick believes the different personalities of his parents contributed to the separation. He characterizes his father as "a laid-back individual [who was] a great mechanic but [a man who was] not good in business." On the other hand, his mother was "aggressive and frugal." Archie and Esther never divorced. Instead, Dick's father moved to New York City while his mother remained in Liberty. The parents decided to send the three boys to the city with Archie. They would attend a school there. Carol would remain with Esther and go to Liberty's central school. In the summers, Al, Arch Jr., and Dick were to return to Liberty. It would have been financially very difficult for Esther to provide for all four of her children if the boys had stayed with her in Liberty. She knew that, but it must have been hard for Esther to agree to a separation from her sons. Perhaps Esther also sensed that her sons could acquire a more advanced education in New York City. Around 1934, then, Dick began to live "a totally different life." Significantly, however, the experience was not a negative one. As Dick concluded, he spent the rest of his youth in "the best of two worlds," New York City during the school year and Liberty in the summer months.

New York City consists of five boroughs, or subdivisions--
Manhattan, the Bronx, Brooklyn, Queens, and Richmond (or Staten
Island). Archie chose to live in the Bronx area, which in the 1930s
was home to almost 1.5 million people.[11] It is the only borough on the
mainland. Basically a residential area, the Bronx is divided into two
parts, the West Bronx and the East Bronx. Three-quarters of the
borough's population lived in the West Bronx, where Jews stood out
as the largest ethnic group.[12] Archie Field rented an apartment in the
East Bronx, which, although described as the "less prosperous
neighbor," had more parks than any of the other boroughs.[13] Archie's
sons could live in close proximity to the undeveloped outdoors they
had grown up in during their childhood in Liberty.

The Field apartment on Beach Street, in the central section of the
East Bronx, was part of a duplex, with a downstairs unit and an
upstairs one. In each unit, residents shared a common kitchen, living
room, and bathroom. Archie and his three boys lived in the upstairs
apartment that consisted of four bedrooms, in addition to the common
areas. Another family, the Ottos, shared the upstairs unit.

Frank and Mary Otto slept in one bedroom,
with their daughter Marie in another. Archie
used the third bedroom. His sons shared the
last bedroom. Dick identifies the neighborhood
as an Irish-Italian one, with a Catholic Church
across the street from the duplex. A family by
the name of von Hagen occupied an apartment
in the building next door to the one where the
Fields lived. Dick became best friends with one
of the sons, Walter, who he met at school. The
von Hagens lived in a two-bedroom apartment.
With seven children, sleeping accommodations were crowded. One of
Walter's siblings was a sister named Anna ("Ann"). Dick defines his
life in New York City as one aspect of "the best of two worlds"
because he met Ann there, the woman who he eventually married.
The two attended grade school together. At first, her parents did not
approve of the young man from Liberty. Dick liked to wear "crazy
hats" that made him stand out. He still has one of those today, a
deerskin hat with a feather at the back of it. (Dick likens it to one

Robin Hood could have worn.) A few years later, Dick did not ingratiate himself with the von Hagens for another reason. He bought a car. Ann's parents realized what that could mean for dates Dick had with their daughter.

The move to New York City meant a new elementary school for Dick. In Liberty, he had attended the central school that went from kindergarten through high school. To complete Dick's education in the lower grades, Archie enrolled him at PS (Public School) 47 on Beach Avenue in the East Bronx. Located just four or five blocks from the Field apartment, Dick walked to school. He went to PS 47 through the eighth grade. Once he graduated from there, Dick went to Haaren High School in Manhattan. Built in 1906, only boys attended that school because of its curriculum. In addition to the traditional academic classes, Haaren specialized in automotive and aviation mechanics courses. It was a vocational school, or what is today known as a technical school. New York State in 1936 only had one hundred vocational and continuation schools; in comparison, the state funded about eleven hundred high schools and academies.[14] The vocational schools had a large student body, enrolling some one hundred thousand students.[15] Given his father's occupation, Haaren proved to be a logical choice for Dick's secondary education years. Looking back, Dick feels he obtained a better education in New York City than he would have received in Liberty because of Haaren. He studied aviation mechanics there. After school, Dick sometimes worked at his father's garage. He could apply some of the technical knowledge he gained in high school there.

Dick rode the subway to Haaren, which was located at Fifty-ninth Street and Tenth Avenue. In so doing, he joined over five million New Yorkers who daily rode the subway.[16] The line Dick took was the IRT, or the Interborough Rapid Transit subway. Blue lamps marked the entrances for the IRT stations. The fare was just five cents. Dick used the subway for other destinations, too. One was the New York Public Library on Forty-second Street and Fifth Avenue. He often went there after school to visit Marie Otto who worked at the library as a telephone operator. Over time, Marie

9

became close with Dick's father, even though she was several years younger than Archie. They never married, in part because Dick's parents never divorced. Marie stayed with Archie until he died in 1968. Even decades later, Dick speaks fondly of Marie. She taught him how to make his way in an adult world, showing him, for example, how to knot a tie and keep his fingernails clean, no easy task for a young man who was mechanical and worked at his father's garage.

But Dick's life in the East Bronx included more than just school and work. He spent hours in Pelham Bay Park, situated in the northeastern section of the borough. With almost two thousand acres, it was the largest park in New York City.[17] He swam in Orchard Beach, located within Pelham Bay. Its facilities must have impressed the young man used to swimming in Liberty's rivers or in Pugley's Creek in his East Bronx neighborhood. Orchard Beach boasted a mile-long strip of white sand. Up to six thousand visitors could use its redbrick bathing pavilion.[18] At first, Dick rode there in a car that belonged to Ann's brother or a cousin. But when he was fifteen, he bought his first automobile, a Model A, for just fifteen dollars. With it, Dick could drive to the Pelham Bay Park as well as to other areas of New York City. He also could take it home to Liberty on holidays or in the summer months. Esther would be there, but so would his brothers. Al did not stay long in New York City; he returned to Liberty. Archie Jr. went back and forth between the East Bronx and his hometown. Only Dick adhered to the plan his parents had agreed upon, namely school years spent in the big city and summers in the small town.

It took about two hours to travel the distance between New York City and Liberty. Dick spent most Thanksgiving vacations and Christmases with Esther. When Dick made the drive to Liberty during his high school years, New York had not yet adopted a maximum speed limit for its highways. But those who drove more than 40 mph for ¼ of a mile could be charged with "reckless driving."[19] When Dick came home in the summer months, at first he tried to go back to his caddying job in Ferndale, but Dick felt too old for that. At one point he worked in a dry cleaning shop in Liberty. For fun, Dick and a

10

few friends drove to nearby swimming holes. The river in Neversink, twelve-feet deep, proved to be a favorite destination. The young men swam and dived in its clear waters.

Yet the cost of gasoline could put a crimp in the pleasure driving of anyone, especially that of high school boys trying to enjoy summer months in rural communities where public transportation was not an option. Dick and his friends came up with a way to acquire some gasoline without buying it. After a paying customer filled his tank at a gas station, a small quantity of fuel remained in the hose. Dick approached the managers at gas stations and asked if he could drain the hoses at the pumps. Hoses at various stations might each yield half a cup or more. Collectively, Dick could acquire a half gallon or more of free gasoline this way. He and his friends also allowed their cars to coast down hills to save on the gasoline.

Dick's car, a Model A

During these visits to Liberty, Dick saw firsthand how hard things were financially for his mother. After she and Archie separated, at one point Esther worked as a chambermaid at a local hotel, then as a seamstress in a dress shop. She also continued to take in roomers. Like most mothers, Esther would have valued the holidays and summer months when all four of her children surrounded her. She might have smiled as she watched her growing boys go off to their swimming holes, just as they had when they were little. The years when Esther could count on having all of her children around her were limited, and she would have known that. One day Carol would marry and move out of the house on Mill Street. As sons, Al, Arch Jr., and Dick would assert their independency much earlier. High school graduation often marked that moment, but for Esther's youngest son, his independence occurred a few months before that rite of passage. By the spring of 1942, Dick was ready to leave the two worlds that had shaped him as a youth. He identifies the outdoor life in Liberty as the best of that world, and his vocational education as well as his relationship with Ann as the best of his New York world. Yet Dick was ready to put both worlds behind him if it meant joining the war effort.

At home in Liberty

He should have graduated from Haaren in June 1942. But as Dick puts it, he was "full of patriotism and wanted to get into the war." So a few months before graduation, Dick dropped out of school, much to the disapproval of his parents. With hindsight, he calls that a "stupid" decision, but at the time it was understandable. Like so many young men of his generation, Dick feared the war would be over before he could enlist. In the spring of 1942, the United States had just entered World War II after the Japanese attack at Pearl Harbor in December 1941. Yet Dick soon found out that enlistment as a seventeen-year-old required his parents' consent, and neither would cooperate. After leaving Haaren, he went home to Liberty. While there, he connected with his friend Chet Slaver. At Chet's urging, the two young men traveled to Messina, New York where they worked at an Alcoa plant on the St. Lawrence River. The cold winter of 1942-1943 prompted Dick and Chet to look elsewhere for employment. They ended up at a construction job at the Navy's Patuxent River Air Station in Maryland. Dick drew on the welding he had learned in vocational school as well as the mechanics his father had taught him. Patuxent A.S. did not open until April 1943. Dick's employment at the Naval station was short-lived. His draft notice arrived in the spring at his official residence on Mill Street in Liberty.

In May, Dick finally found himself where he wanted to be, in the Army. In the infantry, he drew on strengths acquired throughout his youth. Dick knew the outdoors well. He played in it throughout his early years in Liberty, regardless of the season. Swimming, hiking, and hunting were second nature to him. Even during his free time in the East Bronx, he found places where he continued outdoor activities, such as in Pelham Park, Orchard Beach, and Pugsley's Creek. His time outdoors served him even more as the Army put him through the rigorous demands of paratrooper training. Dick believes his years reveling in outdoor pursuits conditioned him for the challenges he confronted in training for the airborne service. The little boy who begged his mother to read *The Little Engine That Could* learned from an early age to persevere in the face of physical challenges. That lesson served him well not only in his military training, but also as he fought in some of the major battles in the European Theater.

Chapter 2

Airborne
"Something different"

With orders to report for induction to Binghamton, New York, Dick drove the eighty miles in his Model A car. Liberty was much too small to be home to an Induction Station, but Binghamton was not. Located near the Pennsylvania-New York border, northwest of Dick's hometown, many industries had factories in Binghamton. It boasted a population of over seventy-eight thousand people on the eve of America's entry into World War II, a number that would have increased because of wartime production by the time Dick arrived there.[20] He spent the day at the Induction Station where he went through a general orientation. The draft board in Liberty had forwarded Dick's paperwork to Binghamton; more pages were added to his file there as a result of some general questions posed to him. The military fingerprinted Dick. He also underwent a medical exam. Dick describes himself then as a "young, macho kid." As such, he had no problem passing the physical. After the medical exam, Dick drove back home to Liberty to await the next orders. Officially, when he left Binghamton he was still a civilian. His next stop in the military's processing system, the Reception Center, would change that status.

Dick recalls that orders arrived within a week. He was to report to Camp Upton on Long Island. A bus line ran from Liberty to New York City. Dick thinks he took an Army bus to the city. A letter to Ann dates his arrival at Upton around the middle of June. She and

Dick's mother saved correspondence they received from him which allows us to accurately date some of Dick's movements. His letters also give the reader insights into his feelings during his months of training. Camp Upton served as a Reception Center for new recruits. Such locations functioned as the second and final step in the transformation of a civilian into a member of the United States military. Dick characterizes the atmosphere at Camp Upton as "chaotic." It must also have been somewhat exciting. An officer swore him and other inductees into the Army. For over a year, Dick planned to join the service. He dropped out of high school to do so. "I wanted to get involved in the war," he recalls, a very common feeling among young men at the time. In an attempt to tailor that involvement to Dick's abilities, he took a general aptitude exam. The men had forty minutes to complete the Army General Classification Test (AGCT). The questions were all multiple-choice. They evaluated the soldier's grasp of basic principles in English and arithmetic.[21]

At the Reception Center, Dick received his first Army supplies. He recalls his uniform basically consisted of a shirt, a pair of pants, socks, and shoes. How the Army issued the uniform resembled an assembly line. Dick and other recruits walked alongside tables piled high with various pieces of clothing. One pile, for example, had shirts, one pants, and one shoes. Soldiers stood on the far side of the tables, looked the inductee up and down to, literally, "size him up." The soldier then gave each man what he estimated to be the proper size clothing. The Army also issued Dick his gear which included a mess kit, knife, rifle, blanket, and a duffle bag with his name stenciled on it. In addition, he received a "shelter half," meaning half of a pup tent. Aside from being "fitted out," as Dick describes it, his military file started to grow. Dick's AGCT results were entered on his Soldier's Qualification Card which already had his educational background on it. After a one-on-one interview, someone entered Dick's hobbies and work experiences on the card. Like the other recruits, he received his first vaccinations and inoculations at Camp Upton's Reception Center. Assembly-line haircuts followed Army specifications. Dick attended what must have seemed like endless orientation sessions to introduce him and other recruits to Army life. NCOs detailed the

15

regulations concerning topics such as pay, allotments, the post exchange (PX) privileges, and leaves. The new soldiers watched movies that showed the dangers of venereal disease. At the Reception Center, Dick also learned how to tell time the Army way.

Probably few inductees who arrived at Camp Upton knew they were waking up at the same Army installation where in World War I songwriter Irving Berlin wrote "Oh! How I Hate to Get Up in the Morning." In the song, a soldier sings a plaintive tune about the early morning call of the bugler. Speaking jokingly for his fellow recruits, he swore, "Someday I'm going to murder the bugler, Someday they're going to find him dead." Just as in World War I, after soldiers woke up in World War II they "fell in," meaning they lined up, ready for the regimentation of the day. They marched and went through hours of physical training. Dick's stay at Camp Upton was not a long one. On a postcard to Ann postmarked June 14, 1943, Dick implies he is anxious to move on to the next level, "I'm still in Upton." He did not have to wait long. The Army put him and other soldiers on a train to Camp Wheeler, outside of Macon, Georgia for three months of Basic Training (BT). They rode "in style," as Dick put it in the postcard, in a Pullman car. He arrived at Camp Wheeler on the afternoon of June 15. The new camp did not impress Dick--"Well, I finally got shipped out of one hellhole right straight into another. Boy it is hot down here."[22]

Postcard sent to Ann on June 14, 1943

Dick was at Camp Wheeler for thirteen weeks, a member of the 1st Platoon in Co. A, 12th Training Battalion.[23] The Army created the camp in 1917 to train National Guard units federalized for World War I service; its use in World War II greatly expanded. At one point, the Army trained over 17,000 recruits there.[24] The day Dick arrived at Camp Wheeler, he shared with Ann his frustration at his current status--"Boy they sure gave me an awful dig. They stuck me right in the dammed infantry. . .The only thing I can try for now is some mechanical line. It will probably be just my luck not to get it."[25] As it turned out, Dick did not get into "some mechanical line." Within two days of his arrival at Camp Wheeler, he volunteered to be a paratrooper, if he could pass the physical and the training.[26] The latter did not begin for a few days.[27] For at least these first days of his time at Camp Wheeler, the summer heat was somewhat easier to endure since physical activity was at a minimum. With average temperatures of 110 to 115 degrees, the recruits received salt pills at every meal.[28] Failure to take them could prove deadly. As Dick explained to Ann, "One fellow went out the other day without his helmet & he had a sun stroke. He hadn't been taking his salt pills…He died the next day. That makes the third one to die from the heat since May."[29]

Dick characterizes his BT at Camp Wheeler as "pretty rigorous," but his life in Liberty prepared him well for some of the demands made on him. The often maligned Drill Instructor (DI), an experienced noncommissioned officer (NCO), moved Dick through BT. This sergeant oversaw the training company to which Dick had been assigned. Dick's DI was "a big, tall Southern guy…a pretty good guy." Dick characterizes him as "laid back." Unlike DIs so often portrayed in Hollywood movies, this sergeant did not use profanity with the recruits. As at Camp Upton, the day began early, at 0500 hours, with reveille.[30] Dick remembers that the men were taught to make their bed so tightly that a quarter could bounce off of it. He made it clear in one letter to Ann how he and others did not countenance those Dick identified as "a bunch of gold brickers." He defined them as recruits who were into "just plain loafing." The way the responsible recruits dealt with such slackers was to "work the fanny right off of those guys whenever we got the chance."[31] Once in formation, the recruits marched to the mess hall for breakfast. The rest of the day included classroom instruction, physical training, and drills.

The fundamentals of their new life--Army life--dominated BT for all of the recruits. The men had been briefly introduced to the world of the military at Camp Upton; that world was explained in more detail at Camp Wheeler. The DI drilled into Dick and others the Army chain of command, how to properly salute, and what constituted the proper care of their gear. Dick particularly remembers the problem of packing the backpack. The mess kit, blanket, shelter half and other items went inside, with the bed roll on the outside. It held so many items that a full one looked "sloppy" in Dick's opinion. This all fell under what could be called "classroom training." Physical fitness exercises proved to be a more crucial factor in BT than textbook training. Calisthenics, with its push-ups, sit-ups, and jumping exercises, served as just a warm-up to much more intense physical conditioning. The rationale behind the physical training was to duplicate conditions encountered in combat situations. Early in July the recruits went out on a nighttime exercise, learning, in Dick's words, "such things as scouting, patrolling, how to sneak up and kill enemy sentries, etc." Around midnight, however, "it started to rain to beat hell." It took three hours to get back to the camp. Dick shared this ordeal with his mother. But probably to put her maternal concerns at ease, he added that the mess crew "had piping hot cocoa & doughnuts waiting for us."[32] Recruits seemed to march and run everywhere. One of their destinations was the camp's obstacle course. A ten-foot-tall tower stood on an edge of a lake. Trainers ordered recruits to jump from the tower and then swim across the lake to another platform. Dick recalls crawling on his belly with live ammo fired over his head. The men also spent hours and hours on the rifle range. Aside from the rifle, they became familiar with machine guns, side arms, and mortars. The recruits learned how to take guns apart and put them back together.

Growing up in Liberty and Neversink prepared Dick for all of this physical training. His life outdoors made it easier for him, for example, to survive the marches and to jump from towers. In his youth, Dick played outdoors, dropping out of trees into the water below. He swam in rivers and went hunting. Going under and around military obstacles became magnified versions of boyhood games, although the barbed wire added a new factor to "playing in the dirt." Skills Dick needed to climb ropes hanging from heights and go down cargo nets had been developed on a more basic level in his youth.[33] That was not true of all recruits. As Dick nonchalantly concludes, "I could handle it [BT]." He points out that physical training posed less of a problem to a country boy like himself than it did to a city boy.

Co-A-12th-Bn-Camp Wheeler Ga, August 1943
Capt. Van Tassall (Commanding)

Just as he drew upon habits learned in his early life to successfully complete forced marches and obstacle courses, Dick built upon boyhood practices when the DI introduced the recruits to weapons training. He had hunted with a rifle in the woods around Liberty. Holding a World War I era bolt-action Springfield rifle, or the newer M1 Garand, did not feel strange to him. It did to those from the city. In a letter to Ann, though, he repeated a warning he had been given, probably by his DI--"They tell me that I'll have to forget all I ever knew about shooting and learn all over again, the army way. That is going to be damned hard to do."[34] Carrying the Garand, which Dick estimated to be over nine pounds, on a five or ten mile hike taxed him.[35] Still, Dick performed so well in BT that the DI singled him out to tutor others. He announced to his mother that, "I'm a coach on the rifle."[36] Dick must have known the pride she would have felt upon reading that. At one point in midday, the recruits returned to the mess hall for lunch. Dinner hours later did not signal the end of the training for that day. Rifles needed to be cleaned and gear stored in the footlocker. The call for "lights out" came after the bugler sounded taps at 2200 hours.[37] Letters to and from his mother and Ann gave Dick a brief respite from the world of the military. After about three weeks at Camp Wheeler, Dick wrote a plea to his mother--"If you find time, I sure would like some cake or cookies or doughnuts [underlined four times] or something."[38] His mother sent packages with home baked items he shared with the other men.

As BT neared its end, perhaps two-three weeks before graduation an airborne captain from Fort Benning, Georgia visited Camp Wheeler. He impressed the recruits in more than one way. The officer explained the basic role paratroopers played in combat operations--they jumped out of an airplane, behind enemy lines. As the captain detailed what the troopers did once on the ground, it became quite apparent to the recruits that airborne troops were part of an elite group. Even their uniform set them apart. On the front of his Class A dress uniform, the officer wore a metal badge that clearly identified him as a paratrooper. The badge took the form of an open parachute with wings on each side. A round, cloth patch with another open chute was on his cap. He wore another cloth patch on his left shoulder. At its center was an airplane with an open parachute underneath it. Above the airplane, at the top of the patch, was the word "Airborne." The young recruits would have noticed the boots even more than the airborne badge and the two patches. At that time, only paratroopers, not other infantrymen, wore boots.

Paratroopers themselves came up with a way to show off their boots. They "bloused" their trousers, meaning they tucked the bottom of their pants into the tops of the boots. The material billowed. Members of airborne units sometimes brought attention to their elite status by calling their fellow infantrymen "straight leg soldiers," or sometimes just a "leg soldier."[39] Paratroopers felt proud of the boots that identified their special status. As such, they polished and polished them. Looking at the captain's boots that day at Camp Wheeler, Dick judged them to be so shiny "you could shave" in them. Paratroopers knew they were special and showed it by the care they took with their uniform, footwear included. Their paycheck also testified to that status. The beginning monthly salary for a soldier was twenty-one dollars. Paratroopers received an additional fifty dollars. Dick remembers the captain pointing that out to the soldiers nearing the end of BT. But Dick explains that it was more than money that moved him to sign up--"I wanted to get involved in something different." It should be emphasized that paratroopers were all volunteers. It took a special type of soldier to risk jumping out of airplanes as a way of fulfilling military service. The trooper had to be more daring than the average infantryman, more sure of himself, too, that he could survive. Out of Dick's company, he estimates that perhaps four or five volunteered with him. But signing up for airborne with the captain that day did not mean Dick or the other recruits would one day wear the uniform of a paratrooper. He first had to make it through parachute training school at Fort Benning.

Once Dick graduated from BT late in September, the Army "shipped" him around, apparently for a few weeks.[40] He finally arrived at Fort Benning where he was ordered to a tent area south of the school, adjacent to Lawson Field, the airport.[41] Usually, recent airborne graduates camped there as they went through additional training.[42] Dick stayed there for awhile as the Army waited for enough volunteers to show up to make a class. Paratroopers called the piece of land "the Frying Pan." Thick woods on hillsides surrounded the area. Streams, the Chattahoochee River, and swamps added to the terrain.[43] It was not so much the concave appearance that earned the area its nickname. The summer temperatures accounted for that. Dick remembers the Georgia clay dirt, the pine needles all over the earth, and daily temperatures "hotter than the devil." While Dick recalls that his introduction to airborne service began in the Frying Pan, the formal jump school experience started when his class was formed. When that happened, Dick and others who had been waiting with him moved to the barracks located on the grounds of the parachute training school.

The school ran for four weeks, with each week designated as a different level in the training program. The first week constituted "A" Stage. All of the exercises were physically demanding. As such, it served as the first opportunity to sort out who could not measure up to the demands placed upon those who wore the uniform of a paratrooper. Dick remembers the first week as calisthenics, drills, rope climbing, forced runs, and push-ups. As he puts it, too, "You ran everywhere." And the sergeant who oversaw the training of each class used even more pushups as punishment for any minor infraction or perceived infraction. Dick points out, "They tried everything to get you to quit." If a trainee could not complete any exercise, he washed out. Dick judges himself to have been "in pretty good physical condition," but "city guys" were not. At the end of the first week, the trainees proved in "A" Stage that they could do a minimum of thirty pushups, climb a thirty-five foot rope, and finish a five-mile run.[44] After a week of such eight-nine hour days, those who were still there moved onto "B" Stage. Each level increased the demands placed upon the paratrooper trainee. Making it through one stage did not guarantee that a trainee would make it through the next stage.

"B" Stage, the second week, continued the physical activities and added ground training to the curriculum. Dick explains that in these seven days trainees learned "the nomenclature of paratroopers," such as airborne's definition of "a stick," the "DZ," and the "opening shock." These all became clear in the week ahead of them. One aspect of "B" Stage that struck Dick was how the classes could have privates and officers in them, yet during this month of training, all of the soldiers took direction from the buck or staff sergeant. That NCO thus gave orders to everyone in the class, including lieutenants, captains, or majors. Dick remembers doing pushups next to a major. Regardless of whether the trainees were enlisted men or officers, the attrition rate was high. Dick thinks it could have been fifty percent.

Jumping from a thirty-four foot tower constituted another part of the "B" Stage curriculum. The trainees dropped from the tower, riding down a pulley to simulate their descent in the air once they left a plane. This exercise washed more than one man out of the program.

The psychological fear of falling got to some of them. The jumper climbed to the top of the tower. There he saw a replica of the C-47's door. Each trainee put on a harness with fifteen-foot long straps that attached to a snap hook with a pulley. A one-hundred-foot steel cable went through the "open door," descending at an angle until it neared the earth. Before the trainee jumped, the instructor attached the hook on the straps to a pulley on the cable. After jumping off of the tower, the trainee slid down the cable until he reached a sawdust pile where he landed.[45] Two of Dick's strong memories of the tower exercise center on the harness he wore and the jerk he felt from the cable.

"C" Stage continued the physical training that characterized "A" Stage and the ground school that marked "B" Stage. There were more tower exercises, but this time with a two hundred and fifty foot tower. Dick spent one entire week jumping off of the high towers.[46] He has a distinct memory of an instructor on the ground, yelling directions through a megaphone. The jumpers also went to a packing shed and learned how to pack a parachute. In a letter to his mother, Dick described the parachute in great detail--"The main chute is 28 ft. in diameter (across the canopy). It has 28 suspension lines. Each line has a tensile strength of 450 lbs. The harness is made of a web material. One thickness of this has a tensile strength of 3000 lbs. The metal fittings are of a cadmium steel. Damned strong. The whole set up is damned strong. Some of the chutes are silk & some nylon. I drew a nylon main chute & a silk reserve."[47] The trainees had jumped from thirty-four foot towers in their second week of training, and now in the third week, they did so from two hundred and fifty foot towers. Dick vividly recalls free falling from a cable that swayed in the wind as he descended. Finally, they were ready to jump from an airplane.

This did not happen until the fourth week, "D" Stage. The prior three weeks were meant to prepare them for these last seven days of parachute training school. The trainer taught the men how to line up in the plane to prepare for the jump, how to exit the plane, how to control the chute after the jump, and, as Dick points out, how to land on the ground without breaking a limb. A C-47 aircraft dropped the trainees over their target.

The sergeant divided the class into "sticks," groups of trainees that numbered around twelve or thirteen. Each stick boarded its own plane. As each trainee climbed aboard, he wore two parachutes, the main one on his back and a reserve chute on his chest. Dick described the reserve chute to his mother, as he had the main chute--"The reserve is 22 ft. in diameter, it has 20 suspension lines."[48] Just above his head, the jumper saw a steel cable that ran down the center of the C-47. A strong string secured a twelve-foot long web strap (known as a static line) to the very top of the canopy on the main chute. The other end of the static line was affixed to a snap hook. The trainee put the hook over the steel cable. As the C-47 neared the drop zone (DZ), the sergeant gave the signal to prepare to exit the plane. In spite of all of the noise from the C-47 that permeated the inside of the plane, the jumpmaster called out a series of brief instructions--"Stand up," "Hook up," "Sound off for equipment check." The jumper behind Dick checked Dick's equipment, and he did that for the paratrooper in front of him. All on board the plane did the same for each other. Each man moved toward the door, pulling his snap hook along the cable. A green light above the door lit up to signal when it was time to jump. He assumed the proper position--feet first, head down, elbows in, knees bent, and hands grasping his reserve chute.

As the trainee went through the open door, the static line became taut, yanking the cover off of the main chute. This action pulled the chute canopy out of its pack. Once the static line was completely stretched out, the string that had fastened the top of the canopy to the static line broke. The static line thus remained secured to the overhead steel cable. This was how it all was supposed to work. But sometimes a trainee had to use his reserve chute. He knew when to pull the cord on his reserve by following a simple counting sequence. As a jumper exited the plane, he was to begin counting, "one thousand and one, one thousand and two, one thousand and three." If the main chute had not opened by that last number, the trainee pulled the cord on his reserve chute.[49] Regardless of what chute unfolded, the jumper felt the "opening shock" when the parachute first unfurled itself. In a vivid description of what it was like to jump from a plane, Dick explained the sensation to his mother--"Boy! Mom, there is nothing like floating through the air in a parachute. It's so soft &

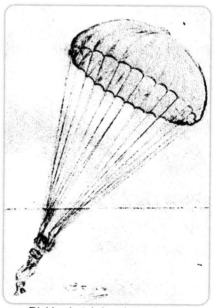

Dick's sketch in a letter home

easy. You feel like you're floating on air (& you are)."[50] Dick learned quickly that he had limited control as he descended, although he could do some maneuvering. He could grab a handful of shroud lines. If Dick pulled down on the front lines, that brought the canopy down and impelled him forward. If he pulled on the back shroud lines, it impelled him backward. Dick could also rotate the canopy by crossing his arms and grabbing the risers, which were wide straps between his shoulder and the shroud lines. The sergeant taught the trainees to fall and tumble upon landing. He stressed, "Never try to stand up when landing."

Dick points to the major requirement of "D" Stage--each trainee had to make five jumps from a plane, with the last one being a night jump. His five did not happen without some quirks. In Dick's first jump, he saw on the ground below him a vehicle with a large red cross painted on its roof, identifying it as an ambulance. It obviously was there in case of an accident with one of the trainees. He admits he felt some "foreboding" on seeing it. On another jump, he sprained his ankle. Looking back decades later, Dick believes that the two most important lessons he learned in those four weeks were how to exit the plane and how to land. He repeats today phrases drummed into him by the instructors--elbows in, hands on each side of the reserve chute, hold your head forward, keep your feet at a forty-five degree angle, and jump feet first. Like Dick, one World War II paratrooper estimates that around fifty percent of those trainees who started in "A" Stage made it all the way through "D" Stage.[51] Put another way, about half of each class washed out.

Dick Field was not one of them. He graduated from Fort Benning's parachute training school on November 27, 1943. An officer pinned wings on Dick's uniform, and he now wore the patches of an airborne trooper. One can easily detect the pride Dick felt in a letter he wrote to his mother dated that same day. He sketched a drawing for her of the wings and arm insignia he now wore. Dick reminded her, and himself, of how hard he had worked for those distinct uniform markings of a paratrooper.[52] The boots issued to him earlier to wear on the training field could now be worn outside of that area and he could "blouse" his pants. Coincidentally, Dick received a package from his mother the morning of graduation. Its timing made it appear to almost be a graduation present. The mailing contained what Dick craved, "homemade cooking," including fudge. He wrote his mother a letter to share graduation day with her and to thank her for the package. Dick ended the letter with a humorous comment that at any other time might have been written in an even more critical tone, but his upbeat mood that day tempered his complaint--"Well, Mom, I guess we are going to fall out soon and hear the Commandant shoot the breeze for awhile. Hear about how Washington stayed at Valley Forge in his bare feet & didn't have anything but tea and sugar. That's his favorite story. The old bat."

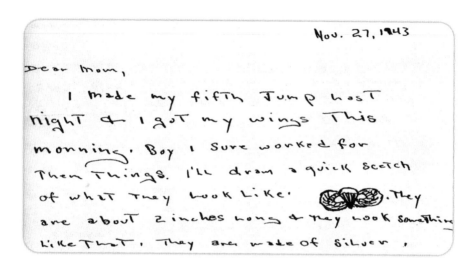

> Nov. 27, 1943
>
> Dear Mom,
>
> I made my fifth Jump last night & I got my wings This morning. Boy I sure worked for Them Things. I'll draw a quick scetch of what They look like. They are about 2 inches long & they look something like That. They are made of silver,

With graduation, Dick became part of an elite group within the infantry. He recalls how some soldiers resented airborne units because paratroopers "thought they were better than everyone else." Yet others "looked at you with respect." And some soldiers "thought you were crazy to jump out of planes." What others thought did not matter to Dick. He volunteered for the airborne because he "wanted to do something different." In less than a week after graduation, Dick received orders to report to Camp Mackall, North Carolina. His wartime service would be "something different" once he became a paratrooper. It also stood out because of the battalion the Army assigned him to.

In December 1943, Dick arrived at his next training stop, Camp Mackall. Located about sixteen miles from Fort Bragg, the Army renamed the camp after the United States entered World War II. It took its new name from Private John Thomas Mackall, the first overseas paratrooper killed in the war when he served in the North

African campaign.[53] A few weeks earlier, the 551st Parachute Infantry Battalion had arrived back in the United States from Panama. There it protected the Caribbean area and supply ships that sailed in those waters.[54] The 551st served in a unique capacity during the war. Battalions usually were attached to a division. The 551st was not. It was one of only two independent parachute units.[55] Its autonomy allowed the military command to move it from one division to another, depending upon the overall strategic need of the moment. At Camp Mackall, Dick and others were assigned to the 551st as replacements. He reported to "B" Company.[56] Arriving at a barracks filled with about one hundred other paratroopers, and knowing none of them, Dick explains that "you learn to make friends." He did so. Over the course of his wartime service, Dick became especially close to Marshall Clay, J.D. Smith, John Kidd, and squad leader Joe Killgore. Together, they endured one last training period before overseas deployment.

At Camp Mackall, the 551st went on twenty-mile forced marches. Dick characterized one to his mother this way--"Boy, that was a killer. I sure as hell slept that night."[57] Another exercise had the paratroopers run for five minutes, then walk for five minutes, with

the actual number of minutes varying. One exercise lasted twenty-four hours. As Dick explained to his mother, they began training that day at 8:00 A.M. and proceeded to practice attacks "all day and night. We were digging foxholes and anything else to make it miserable for us." The cold night followed the warm day. In spite of how demanding the training was, Dick clearly relished what he was doing. "I like this outfit, as tough as it is. They are a swell bunch of fellows." [58] In addition to the continued physical training, Dick remembers "a lot of weapons training." The men spent hours on the firing range. As expected, members of the 551st made more parachute jumps. Some of them were what Dick calls "Hollywood jumps," meaning the men carried no equipment, just the chute. Also, not all of their training jumps were from airplanes with engines. The Army wanted to try having some paratroopers jump from gliders. If this could be done without too many problems, it had advantages for airborne units. The absence of a propeller blast allowed the jumpers to descend almost vertically. The glider could thus help the men land as one compact unit, not spread across a wide area as they would be in a traditional jump from a plane.[59] The high command used the 551st at Camp Mackall to evaluate the effectiveness of this idea. Dick became part of this experiment when all of the men in Company B volunteered for some of these jumps.

For Dick, the first one occurred on December 7, 1943. He drew his mother's attention to that date in a letter he wrote her five days later. Dick reminded her that the Japanese attack at Pearl Harbor two years earlier now coincided with a proud moment for him and others in the 551st. As he described the event, "I was with a group of fellows & we were the first ones to jump with full equipment from a glider. We jumped from those troop carrying gliders. It's never been done before. I sweated out the ride in the dammed glider more than I did the jump."[60] Dick judged the gliders to be "much worse than the planes. You see, they fly at such low altitudes and there are lots more air currents the lower you get, so it's quite bumpy at around 1,000 feet."[61] Today, Dick still vividly recalls a C-47 that towed two gliders, with twelve men in each, Dick being one of them. The "flimsiness" of the gliders struck him. (The troops called them "the flying coffins."[62]) Instead of one exit door, a glider had two, one on each side of the plane. Dick explains that the doors were so low that the paratroopers had to "duck walk" when jumping out. Jumpers had to take turns exiting out of first one side, then the other, to guard against the glider tipping.[63] Dick made at least two if not three jumps from a glider. Another one was before several important government officials visiting from Washington D.C., including Secretary of War

Harry Stimson. In making these test jumps from gliders, the 551st made history. The Army recognized the battalion by bestowing on it an official United States Army commendation. One major general cited "the fine spirit" of the men, "which prompted many volunteers to hazard tests in parachute jumping of a type which had not been done before."[64]

Dick on left in glider exercise

Dick spent Christmas, the first one away from his family, at Camp Mackall. He did not want for attention, however. A few days before the 25th, he received a package from his mother that contained film for his camera and woolen socks. In a letter to her dated December 26th, Dick detailed the bounty of other gifts he received from family and friends. His brother Al gave him twenty dollars. Aunt Fannie and Uncle Clyde mailed a Yardley shaving outfit as a present. From other relatives Dick received nuts, candy, cigarettes and some small books he could carry in his pocket. Friends in Liberty sent him "more Christmas cards than I'll ever be able to answer." Perhaps to put his mother's mind at ease, Dick informed her that he had "been going to church down here quite regularly. I guess Mrs. Field's little boy Dickie is reforming."[65]

During the 1943 Christmas season, Dick bought himself a second pair of the boots only paratroopers wore. In a letter to her son, Mrs. Field referred to the care someone told her that jumpers gave to their boots. After verifying that what she heard was correct, Dick described it in detail to his mother. "We saddle soap them when they get wet so that they will keep soft & won't crack. They have to be soft or they will raise hell with your feet. There is quite a lot of work to breaking in a new pair. You take & soak them in a tub of water till they get good & soaked. Then we saddle soap the devil out of them. Then we put them on & wear them around till they are dry. That way they wear right in to the shape of your foot. When they are dry we rub in another coat of saddle soap & then polish them…We polish them with ox blood [the name given to a deep maroon color of shoe polish] or mahogany polish so they get nice and dark."

Aside from the glider jump, Dick and other members of the 551st participated in a second historic event for their battalion at Camp Mackall. This one, however, was of a tragic nature. Because of a poorly planned night jump, eight paratroopers died in a training exercise on February 16, 1944. Today, almost seventy years after the accident, Dick begins telling the story by sharing perhaps the major reason why it happened. The high command replaced Lieutenant Colonel Wood Joerg, the Commanding Officer (CO) of the 551st, with Lieutenant Colonel Rupert Graves. Like others who have told this story, Dick refers to it as "the Kinney Cameron jump" because of the lake the paratroopers landed in. And, like others who recount the details of the jump, he blames Graves for the loss of lives. The men of the 551st had confidence in Joerg's leadership abilities. He had proven his skills during their time in Panama. Joerg also accepted rather than fought the maverick nature of the men in his battalion. But late in October 1943, less than two months after the Army assigned Dick to the battalion, Graves replaced Joerg who was transferred to a high post in a newly formed regiment. Graves made it clear at the outset that he would not countenance any questionable behavior from the 551st. He appeared almost determined to break the somewhat rebellious will of the men, ordering exercises that seemed more like punishments than physical conditioning. Graves demanded long marches in freezing temperatures, abolished furloughs, reduced the number of NCOs, and ordered solitary confinement as punishment for minor infractions.[66] By February 1944, a palatable tension existed between the new CO and the men under him, one of whom was Dick

31

Field. As Dick sums up the feeling of the 551st toward Graves, "The guys had no respect for the colonel."

The 551st did two night jumps at Camp Mackall. The fateful one on February 16, 1944 was its first. The new CO showed poor judgment from the very beginning of the exercise when he chose the DZ. Graves selected a narrow peanut and corn field between Broad Acres Lake to the north and Lake Kinney Cameron to the south. Both bodies of water were just a few miles east of Camp Mackall. The landing field measured just sixteen hundred feet in width and two thousand feet in length. Thirty-one C-47s were to drop six hundred and fifty paratroopers onto the DZ. With such a narrow strip, even experienced pilots would have been challenged to drop the men on target. And these pilots were not experienced. Those who flew the C-47s that February night had never been part of a parachute drop, and their time practicing for this one proved minimal.[67] In a letter he wrote the evening after the disastrous jump, Dick scorned the Air Corps crews for their role in the training exercise. Probably because the Army could have severely disciplined him if his letter became public, Dick did not mention Graves.

By their very nature, night drops are dangerous. Adverse weather conditions added to the risk. Dick remembers the sky as overcast, with mist in the air. He is not alone in thinking that Graves should have aborted the drop for that night. The 551st boarded the C-47s at Polk Airfield, adjacent to Fort Bragg. While waiting to go on the transport plane, Dick went over to a table laden with donuts and coffee. He added sugar to his cup, not realizing that the coffee already had the sweetener in it. Once Dick took a sip, he realized what had happened, but seeing the long line to get a new cup, he just drank from the one he had. Dick recalls a bumpy 7:00 P.M. take-off for his transport plane.[68] After about thirty minutes in the air, Dick felt the coffee, which he describes as feeling like "a lead weight" in his stomach, coming up on him. The close quarters in the C-47 aggravated his discomfort. Dick vomited, with his breakfast running down the aisle as the rest of his stick looked on. "I was not the most popular guy in the place," Dick admits. His unit was scheduled to jump at 8:30 P.M.; at 8:15 they "stood up & hooked up. We came over the field but we didn't get the signal to jump in time so we had to swing around again."[69] This second time the pilot did not use the correct approach to the DZ; as Dick wrote the very next day, "The dumb air corps jerks didn't come back over the field on the same azimuth so the[y] didn't even hit the damned field. They got us way down over the woods..." [70] The Air Corps "gave us the go signal anyway so out we went. We didn't even know that we weren't over the field."[71] In Dick's words, the moonless night "was very dark." As he dropped down through the sky in his chute, Dick thought he spotted the DZ. It stood out as a piece of land that from above appeared darker than the surrounding area. But in a letter written the next day, Dick admitted "it was so dark that you couldn't see where you were going at all. The guys were landing in the trees all over."[72] Dick heard splashing as he descended. Because of some maneuvering he did on his descent, Dick landed about ten-fifteen feet from the edge of Lake Kinney Cameron. He barely missed the water. Dick knew, however, from the sound he heard coming down, that others had not been so lucky. After he got his harness off, Dick waded into the lake to help some of the trainees who had landed in it.

About forty members of the 551st fell into the lake. Each jumper carried between seventy-five to one hundred pounds of equipment. Some landed in shallow water. For those who were not that lucky, the weight pulled men under deep water. Seven hundred and twenty feet of tangled lines that connected the parachute to the harness made it difficult for some to disconnect themselves from the chute. Eight of the men could not free themselves. Seven bodies were recovered without too much difficulty, but not the eighth one. Dick explains that the parachute belonging to one of the men who died had become entangled in a stump at the bottom of Kinney Cameron. On the 17th, Army personnel drained the lake all day in order to retrieve the bodies.[73] One of those who drowned was a corporal in Dick's platoon, Benjamin Preziotti.[74] A Catholic mass on the night of the 17th was said for those who died, and Dick attended.[75] After the religious service, he wrote a three-page letter to his mother, fearful that she would read stories about the training accident in a newspaper and worry about Dick. In it, he shared specific details of the night jump and its aftermath. Understandably, Dick told his mother that he had landed "in a small clearing." He purposely lied to her about how close he had been to the lake. In addition to those who died, Dick told his mother that out of five hundred paratroopers who jumped that evening, sixty-one suffered various injuries, with eight broken legs "and the rest were sprains or cuts." Over the years, details such as these would be lost in his general recollections of the Kinney Cameron jump. The main story of what happened that night, however, would never be forgotten by Dick and the other paratroopers. Decades later, in 1992, the men of the 551st who survived that jump paid for the erection of a memorial to the eight who died. It stands at Camp Mackall, about fifteen to twenty feet from Kinney Cameron Lake. About a month after the accident, the Army transferred Graves out of the 551st to another parachute regiment. Joerg returned to again assume command.

During his time at Camp Mackall, Dick went on leave to visit Ann and his family. A humorous chain of events marked one trip back to New York. Dick and his friend John Castellano, who was from the West Bronx, got a three-day weekend pass. The challenge was to get to New York City from North Carolina as fast as possible. The two friends went to an airport at Camp Mackall. They planned to hitch a ride on a military plane to New York City. Once at the airport, however, Dick and John were told to check out a parachute for the plane ride, which they did. Hours passed before space became available for them on a departing flight. It turned out to be on a plane destined for West Virginia, via an airport that was right near that state's border, but in Ohio. When Dick and John landed in Ohio, they realized that this detour put them further away from New York City than they had been before they left Camp Mackall. They made their way to Huntington, West Virginia where they sought out the Red Cross or the United Service Organization (USO). Dick is not sure which agency helped them, but one did. He and John received money to purchase train tickets to New York City. When they arrived at Penn Station, the two soldiers stood out from all of the other men in uniform because of the parachute each carried. As Dick explains, he and John "had checked it out, so we had to keep it to check it back in." Dick saw his father and Ann, but he only had about one hour with each. His father gave him money for the train trip back to North Carolina. Dick arrived at Camp Mackall about six-seven hours late based on the time indicated for his leave on the three-day pass. In those hours, Dick was officially AWOL (absent without official leave). His punishment took the form of "an arrest to quarters" for one week, which Dick explains as "one step below the brig."

As this one attempt illustrates, spending time with Ann proved difficult given Dick's military service. The two talked about marriage before Dick left for his induction. Originally, they decided not to get married until the war ended, but Dick changed his mind when he was based at Camp Mackall. As he puts it simply and powerfully, "I worried that I might not come back [from the war]." Early in 1944, Dick wrote Ann, asking her to join him in North Carolina so they could marry. On the back of the envelope, he wrote specific instructions for her on how to get to Camp Mackall--"Take train to Hamlet, N.C. Take bus from Hamlet to Camp Mackall. Ask for guest house. You tell me the time to meet you."[76] Dick was nineteen, Ann eighteen. In the Bronx, they had spent their teen years together. Dick saw her then as "one of the guys." In those years, Dick and Ann found

35

out that they shared similar likes and dislikes as well as similar values. Dick also points to Ann's appearance. She was unquestionably "good looking." Dick followed up on his earlier proposal in a Western Union telegram with a handwritten date of "March 26" on the front of its envelope. The telegram was short and to the point--"ANN TAKE 1005 AM TRAIN SUN OR MON TO HAMLET URGENT."[77] In response, Ann took a train to North Carolina late in March. That state had a waiting period, but South Carolina did not. With Camp Mackall near the state border, the two drove in a borrowed car to Bennettsville, South Carolina. After paying the required five dollars, a justice of the peace married them on March 29, 1944. They spent their honeymoon at the Hotel Powers in Bennettsville. Afterwards, Ann found a room for them in a private home in Rockingham, North Carolina, not far from Camp Mackall. Other married members in the 551st also rented a room there. Together, the troopers carpooled daily from the camp to the one-room home they shared with their wives. Ann stayed in Rockingham until shortly before Dick left the States.

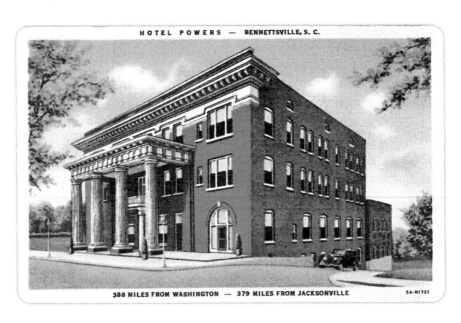

HOTEL POWERS — BENNETTSVILLE, S. C.

388 MILES FROM WASHINGTON — 379 MILES FROM JACKSONVILLE   5A-H1721

It had been one year since Dick's draft notice arrived at his childhood home in Liberty, New York. In those months, Dick had been inducted, processed, put through Basic Training, volunteered for airborne service, and survived rigorous training as a paratrooper at first Fort Benning and then Camp Mackall. Given the role of the airborne, Dick knew he was shipping out soon to the European Theater. (Only one airborne unit, he points out, ended up in the Pacific Theater.) As it turned out, Dick and Ann had just about two weeks together. In a letter to his wife dated April 11, 1944, Dick explained, "Well Hon, this will be the last letter that I write to you uncensored. I guess you know what that means. We are restricted after 5:30 tomorrow morning. We are really hot now. It won't be very long."[78] He shipped out in April. Dick had already set up an allotment for his mother that directed to her a portion of his monthly paycheck. He arranged a second one now for his wife. Each woman received a fifty dollar check every month. The Army deducted twenty-two dollars of that amount from Dick's paycheck, and the government contributed the other twenty-eight dollars.[79] Dick also bought the maximum life insurance the military offered to its troops, $10,000. In his professional life as a soldier, and in his personal life, Dick was as prepared as he could be for the combat he knew he would see.

Chapter 3

North Africa, Sicily, and Italy
"Anxious to get into it"

In the months after his arrival in the European Theater of Operations (ETO), the combat Dick had trained for over the course of eleven months eluded him. The 551st moved from one area of the Mediterranean zone to another in the spring and summer of 1944, but the locations were ones the Allies had already secured. The 551st landed in North Africa eighteen months after the Americans and British had taken it from German forces. From there the battalion went to Italy, specifically to Naples, Sicily, and Rome. Naples had been secured in October 1943 and Sicily a few months earlier. Dick and his fellow paratroopers arrived in Rome about a month after the Allies had taken the city in June 1944. The 551st spent July in the area. It was not until August 1944 that Dick and his battalion saw combat. They became part of the invasion of southern France, code-named Operation Dragoon. When asked about the months leading up to Dragoon, Dick readily admitted that by August, and even before, he was "anxious to get into it." And "get into it" he did. Fighting in southern France was followed by combat operations in the Maritime Alps, in Belgium during the famous Battle of the Bulge, and then more confrontations with enemy forces as the paratroopers made their way into Germany with the rest of the Allied forces. Up through the Battle of the Bulge, his unit identification was 2nd Squad, 2nd Platoon, Company B of the 551st Parachute Infantry Battalion.

Throughout his time in the ETO, Dick wrote letters to his wife and mother, just as he had during BT and paratrooper training. Due to wartime censorship, the correspondence could not detail his military experiences as had his letters written stateside. They do contain one refrain that must have brought a smile to Ann and Esther--"Do not worry about me," he urged his wife and mother. Even as he made this request, Dick must have known that they both would do so, with good reason. By war's end, paratroopers in the 551st experienced "the longest consecutive stretch of combat by any U.S. Airborne unit" in the European Theater.[80]

On its way to the ETO, the 551st first stopped for a week at Camp Patrick Henry in Newport News, Virginia. Dick is quite clear in his recollection that his battalion did not undergo additional training here. The Army base, located in 1,700 woodland acres that could have lent itself to military exercises, served as a staging area for troops shipping out to the war zone. Recreation halls, Service Clubs, and theaters at the camp were just some of the ways the 551st could pass the days. At night, Dick remembers the paratroopers sleeping in tents. By the end of the war, almost one and a half million members of the armed forces passed through Camp Patrick Henry.[81] The 551st, which numbered less than a thousand, constituted just a small percentage of them. From the camp, the battalion went to the docks at the Hampton Roads Port of Embarkation (P.O.E.) for two nights.[82] Dick believes the 551st probably slept in mess tents at the dock. His battalion shipped out on April 22, 1944, eleven days after he wrote his last uncensored letter to Ann until Germany surrendered in May 1945. Security was tight, as in all war-related departures. The military worked to keep troop movements within the United States as secret as possible. Dick remembers one incident as the paratroopers prepared to board their ships. The government appears to especially have wanted to keep secret the fact that some of the soldiers were airborne. One of the men in the 551st had a large tattoo of parachute wings on his chest. With amusement, Dick recalls that officers ordered the jumper to cover the wings with pieces of tape. He is sure the camouflage was temporary, just for the boarding process. What Dick recounts so vividly about the departure relates to what he saw that April 22nd. As he describes the sight, "Everywhere you looked, you could see nothing but ships."

The three vessels the 551st Parachute Infantry Battalion sailed on were part of a convoy identified as UGS-40, and as Dick points out, "A convoy is only as fast as the slowest ship." His convoy was a large one and his ship a slow one. The convoy sailed with flags from five nations--the United States (which registered the majority of the ships), Britain, Canada, Norway, and the Netherlands. Because vessels joined and left the convoy at various points, the exact number in UGS-40 cannot be ascertained. Approximately sixty-five Merchant Marine ships sailed in it, as did eighteen American, British, and French military ships that made up Naval Task Force 61. Factoring in about ten additional ships whose names were not recorded, the convoy was composed of almost one hundred vessels.[83]

Along with others in Company B, Dick was on board the *USS William Mulholland*, a Liberty ship with its hull number, 0677, painted on its bow. Dubbed "the Model T of the seas" by one person, the mass-produced Liberty ships became the backbone of the American and British merchant fleets.[84] Company A joined Dick's unit on the *Mulholland*. The rest of the 551st was assigned to two other Liberty vessels.[85] The government named the 2,751 Liberty ships after deceased Americans. Any group that raised two million dollars for war bonds could suggest a name for a Liberty ship.[86] In all probability, Los Angeles residents collected money that built the *William Mulholland* since its namesake had been the head of the Los Angeles Department of Water and Power. He brought water from the Owens Valley to L.A. in 1913, thus assuring an adequate water supply for the metropolitan area. Dick recalls the *William Mulholland* as a "full ship," packed with men and equipment. It could carry five hundred and fifty troops. As with all Liberty ships, this one measured four hundred and forty-one feet in length and fifty-six feet in width. Its five holds could carry over nine thousand tons of cargo. Airplanes and tanks could be tied to its deck.[87] Dick remembers seeing planes on his Liberty ship. The *William Mulholland's* three-cylinder, reciprocating steam engine ran the ship at a speed of 11 knots.[88]

It took UGS-40 three weeks to reach the Mediterranean. Rather than maintain a linear approach, Dick points out that the ships zigzagged, to avoid German attacks, as they neared European waters. That, as well as the slow speed of the Liberty ships, also contributed to the lengthy voyage. In those weeks, meals basically consisted of spam and chili.[89] The men took saltwater showers, a new experience for the vast majority of them.[90] One memory that Dick likes to share regarding the trip across the Atlantic is the fact that he learned to play cribbage on board the ship, a game he still enjoys today. He points out that the weather in April was good, allowing the soldiers to play cards topside, under the deck covers. Throughout the voyage across the Atlantic, the paratroopers in the 551st participated in several drills in case of an enemy aerial attack as they approached Europe. Dick recalls lifeboat drills as part of these exercises, although he judges them to have been "worthless" if an attack occurred because the small boats could not have held all of the men on board the ship. As it turned out, such enemy action took place, but it did not directly involve the *William Mulholland*. On May 9th UGS-40 sailed through the Straits of Gibraltar. Dick remembers how, as the ships approached Gibraltar "in broad daylight," he saw a "peak sticking out of the water." The sheer size of the convoy especially brought it to the attention of German forces in the Mediterranean. Sixty-two enemy aircraft, with fighter cover, went after UGS-40 on the night of May 11th as it approached the coast of North Africa. One World War II Naval veteran judges the German action to have been "the most intensive air attack on any convoy in this arena over the second half of WW2."[91] Some Allied planes based in the area went to the defense of UGS-40. Still, the enemy planes dropped an estimated ninety-two torpedoes and other bombs.[92] Dick knows that at least one ship that carried members of his battalion sustained some damage. It was diverted to Gibraltar for repairs. Men on it joined the rest of the 551st about a week later. But on the night of the 11th, troops on the *William Mulholland* remained oblivious to the attack. Dick thinks he heard about the incident after the 551st arrived in North Africa.

Eighteen months earlier, Allied forces had first landed there as they began to wrest control of North Africa away from the European

41

Axis powers. The Allies successfully reclaimed the area in November 1942 in a major campaign called Operation Torch. The *William Mulholland* unloaded its cargo, including the 551st Parachute Infantry Battalion, on May 12th in Oran, Algeria. Next to the city of Algiers, Oran was "the greatest seaport on the old Pirate Coast."[93] Fittingly, the 551st first touched land in the ETO at a location that had been the site of the first American airborne operation of World War II, part of Operation Torch.[94]

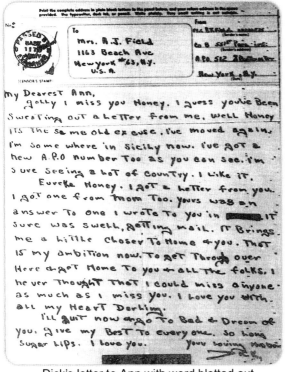

Dick's letter to Ann with word blotted out.

Dick's battalion lived in a tent camp about five miles out in the desert at Merze el-Khebir.[95] They slept in squad or pyramidal tents, as Dick explains, with ten men in each one, five on one side of the tent and five on the other side. According to Dick, "not a lot of training" occurred in Oran. He thus had time to write to both Ann and Esther. Two factors, however, resulted in letters that were much shorter than ones he had written while in BT and paratrooper training. The first concerned military censorship. Designated officers in Army units read each piece of correspondence enlisted soldiers wrote. Understanding that the mail could be compromised, the censor blotted out, and at times cut out, any references to location, unit designations, or phrases the censor thought could give the enemy information on troop movements. As Dick explained to Ann in a May 11th letter, he was "somewhere in North

Africa but I can't say anymore than that." He could not include detailed descriptions of the area the 551st was in or plans for the battalion's immediate movements.

The second factor that resulted in Dick's letters being shorter concerned his use of a new format for correspondence known as V-Mail. (The alphabetical letter designated the much-used Allied goal of "victory.") Letters originating either on the Home Front or in an overseas war theater were reduced both in size and weight. The Signal Corps microfilmed the correspondence written on a government-supplied sheet of paper that measured seven and a half inches by seven and three quarters inches. The resulting film roll was then sent to the Home Front, or overseas, where the Signal Corps printed the V-Mail on smaller, lightweight photo paper for delivery to the addressee.[96] This dramatically reduced the space bags of mail took up in transit, allowing for as much cargo room to be used for military equipment as possible. Dick chose to use V-Mail for some of his letters. He believes that "the high command suggested" this method of letter-writing to make room for more military cargo. In addition to using the V-Mail format, Dick also wrote letters on Army stationery (which displayed an eagle at the top of each page), smaller pieces of plain paper, and sometimes American Red Cross stationery. Regardless of what he wrote upon, Dick recalls that the sheets and postage were free to the troops.

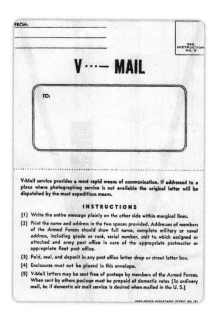

Three strong memories Dick carries of his brief time in North Africa center on the natives, swarms of locusts, and mutton (sheep meat). In a letter to his mother postmarked May 24, 1944, Dick summarized, perhaps with an understatement, his impression of the indigenous people in Oran--"The natives here are real interesting." Their dress, unlike any clothing Dick had ever seen in the states, struck him. The baggy pants Arab men wore, tight at the ankles, reminded him of the trousers in an outfit some young American men wore. In the States, it was known as a "zoot suit." Dick referred to the Arab garb in a May 11, 1944 letter to Ann as "the damdest zoot suits you have ever seen." With amusement, he also saw how some inventive children exchanged their native garb for one that clearly bore the mark of the American Army. Dick shared that image, too, with his wife--"It seemed funny to see an Arab kid walking down the street with some G.I.'s barracks bag on for a pair of pants and see [the name] John Smith written across his butt."[97] But Dick found out that it might not have been a good idea to draw conclusions about the natives based only on their dress, which to some might have appeared "backward." He had been assigned guard duty, which, Dick explained to his wife, gave him a chance to speak to some of the Arabians. One was "Benny," a thirteen-year-old who spoke six different languages. The boy clearly impressed the New Yorker who, in his area of the Bronx, heard Italian spoken but did not understand it. As Dick wrote in a V-Mail letter postmarked May 24, 1944, "Boy is he a smart little devil. He can sing 'Whatch know Joe, lay that pistol down,' play poker, casino, Black Jack & any number of other things."

A second vivid recollection Dick has of his stay in Oran centers on the locusts. Natives in the local vineyards spent much effort, according to Dick, trying to get the insects away from the grapes. He remembers "hoards of locusts" flying around. Moving about was, he points out, "like walking through a cloud of locusts," slipping as he went. Mutton remains a vivid, last memory Dick carries with him for that short stay in Oran. While the main ingredient for wine lay in the vineyards around them, the paratroopers drank milky tea served with mutton while in Algeria.[98] According to Dick, the mutton was "strong tasting." After ten days in Oran, the 551st boarded a British troop carrier.[99] Dick remembers that "the whole ship smelled of mutton." Contributing to his memory may be the fact that many paratroopers suffered from severe diarrhea on their trip across the

Mediterranean.[100] Dick points out that the troop ship was not equipped with bunks. The men rested on hammocks hung in the lower levels of the vessels. They did not have to stay long on board, however. The ship docked at Naples on May 23, 1944, putting the 551st on the European continent for the first time.[101]

In a letter to Ann written on May 24, 1945, exactly one year and one day after this landing, Dick shared with her his impressions of Naples. He could be free in writing these because the Army ceased its censorship of letters since Germany had surrender. As Dick described the city he found in May 1944, "...it was one hell of a mess. The harbor was full of sunken ships and the docks and city were just a mess of rubble. Oran wasn't shot up too bad but at Naples I first saw poverty & [the] devastation that war brings." By the time the 551st arrived in that city, eight months had passed since British forces first landed at the southernmost tip of Italy early in September 1943. They began an Allied movement north that became known as "up the bloody boot," a reference to both the shape of Italy on a map and the heavy casualties Allies suffered. For well over a year, American and British forces fought the Germans as they "climbed" that boot from its southern-most tip to its northern border with Switzerland and Austria. In fact, the Allies did not reach those borders until the very week Germany surrendered early in May 1945. It thus took nineteen months to climb the boot. The destruction Dick witnessed in Naples was just the beginning of a long period of the war fought on Italian soil. One lasting memory Dick has of his brief stay in the city was the sight of Mount Vesuvius on the Bay of Naples. He had just missed a major display of its power. In March 1944, two months before the paratrooper battalion arrived there, a two-week long eruption of Mount Vesuvius occurred, complete with a lava flow and explosions.[102] After a few days in Naples, the 551st boarded boxcars for a train trip to southern Italy.

Known as "40 and 8s," a reference to their capacity to carry either forty men or eight horses, the boxcars became a common transportation method for American soldiers. Dick points out that there were no toilet accommodations on the boxcars, nor was water stored on the cars. The soldiers drank from their canteens or used water stored in "jerrycans," large metal containers used to carry extra gasoline at the back of a jeep. On the boxcars, they held water. The trip from Naples to the very tip of "the boot" took about a week. Along the way, members of the 551st traded with Italians they met when the train stopped. The Americans exchanged ration items, in particular cigarettes and candy, for local foods, such as tomatoes, eggs, and especially wine. Dick participated in this bartering, using his C rations and cigarettes to obtain some wine and fruit. (The Army issued C rations and K rations to its troops in the field. C rations were mostly canned food. Dick remembers about four or five cans, with franks and beans being the most popular. The Army also distributed K rations. These were less bulky since they were three small boxes. Dick recalls some of the items in K rations as being cheese, crackers, a chocolate bar, cigarettes, and even toilet paper.)

In the course of the train ride south, soldiers consumed the food items they bartered from the local inhabitants. The troopers had a portable stove they used for food preparation. The wine obtained from the natives along the way must have especially made the journey a more pleasant one. As they made their way south, Dick remembers the men bathing in the waters of the Mediterranean when the train stopped near beaches. Once they arrived at Reggio de Calabria, located at the "toe" of the Italian peninsula, ferries took the 551st to the island of Sicily. To do so, the battalion journeyed across the Straits of Messina, a narrow body of water between the eastern tip of Italy and Sicily.[103] Dick describes himself and his fellow paratroopers as "elated" when they first arrived at the Straits, thinking that they were done with the boxcars. But as it turned out, Dick explains that for the trip across the water, "they never got off the boxcars." The ferry had railroad tracks on it, and the boxcars went straight onto those tracks.

Sicily's appearance shocked Dick, as had Naples, but in a different way. Compare Dick's observation on Sicily in a letter to Ann written while he was on the island with one written almost a year later when the Army no longer censored letters. On June 15, 1944, Dick simply concluded to Ann, "This is quite a nice place." On May

24, 1945, he observed to Ann, "Well, Sicily was the filthiest country I've ever been in. It seemed like civilization was lost when you crossed [the Strait of Messina]."[104] Dick saw his second volcano while on Sicily. As the ferry traveled across the Straits, he watched the smoke and steam rise from the island's Mount Etna.

The 551st stayed in Sicily throughout the month of June. The battalion bivouacked at Camp Wright, near Trapani, on the western coast. The camp was located outside of the city, in a countryside where Dick vividly recalls the orchards of trees laden with blood oranges. They were in transit to that destination when word reached them that the Allies had captured Rome. Two days later, the June 6th landings at Normandy occurred.

The 551st set up a parachute school for French and Polish soldiers.[105] Although Dick did not help to train the Allied jumpers, he does remember the death of a French paratrooper who did not hook up his static line. Additional training occupied members of the 551st. Dick remembers "a lot" of  exercises. At Camp Wright, the paratroopers spent a considerable amount of time on the rifle range, shooting, as Dick recalls, .45 pistols, rifles, machine guns, and mortars. He points out that the men fired from the beach into nearby cliffs so that "the bullets would not fly all over." Part of the training included forced marches into nearby mountains. On one night march, Dick slipped from a trail and fell into a gully, spraining his knee "quite badly." After being evacuated in a jeep, a medic or doctor put him on aspirin. There was no nearby Army hospital, so Dick followed the medical advice of just staying off the foot for several days. (Years later, he received a knee replacement because of this training accident.)

As in Oran and Naples, Dick was sensitive to the living conditions of the local population. In a letter to Ann dated June 15,

1944, he noted how "the people have a hard time getting cigarettes and soap here. You can get six oranges for a dime or 50 of them for a pack of cigarettes." Dick then went on to detail what American soldiers paid for some goods and services. A quart of wine cost about fifty cents, a handkerchief one penny as did a pair of socks, a blanket was a dime. A shave or a haircut a nickel, the same charge for laundering "a suntan shirt or a field jacket." As he concluded to Ann, "pretty cheap living expenses, eh?" To illustrate the economy in a tangible way, in this same letter Dick mailed his wife some French francs and Italian liras. He explained that one hundred francs were worth two United States dollars while one lira equated to only one cent. He also enclosed a five dollar American bill. It was one his father had mailed him in care of the P.O.E. back in Virginia. Dick told Ann that the money "just caught up with me." After having "some of the guys sign it," he now forwarded it to Ann. As he pointed out to her, the five-dollar bill had "been half way around the world." Dick clearly expected Ann to keep the bill because of all the signatures on it, but in this same letter he told her that a few days earlier he had received his monthly pay. From it, he mailed her sixty dollars in cash. Dick also had filled out an updated allotment form to increase her monthly amount by twenty dollars.

Thoughts of home were always with Dick, and this is especially evident in the June 15th letter. That summer, Ann made her first trip to Liberty, to meet Esther and Carol. Dick, of course, knew Mrs. von Hagen very well since he had lived in the Bronx. Ann, though, had never met Dick's mother or sister. The month before, for Mother's Day, he had sent flowers to both his own mother and then to Ann's, who was now his mother-in-law. The gesture touched his bride, to which Dick replied, "I felt it was the least I could do. I'm sorry I could not give them to her personally." He naturally wished he could have accompanied Ann on her first visit to his childhood home. Even though Dick knew his family would receive his wife with open arms, there were parts of Liberty he wanted to share with her--"I could have shown you the old swimming hole & wood[s] where I used to hunt & a lot of other things."

Like all of those who served during the war, Dick missed home and family. He carried around a lengthy poem, probably clipped from the G.I. newspaper, *Stars and Stripes*. The poem's title explains its importance to Dick, "Litany for Homesick Men." Written by a corporal in New Guinea, it refers to the sights and sounds of home such as subways in New York City, "the El conductor in Chicago," small restaurants, "sleepy streets," a cabin in the woods, and "tall apartments in Yonkers." Much more than these places, Dick and others in uniform missed their loved ones. For Dick, this was especially true when it came to Ann. The newlyweds had had only a few weeks together before he shipped out. In a letter from Sicily dated June 17, 1944, Dick explained his "ambition," as he defined it--"To get through over here & get home to you and all the folks. I never thought that I could miss anyone as much as I miss you." About a month later, after the 551st left Sicily to return to Italy, Dick hinted at how

sometimes his exasperation at the distance between them affected his temperament--"Golly Honey, I love you and miss you so damned much. I've sure got to cut loose on somebody for all of the Hell I've gone through. I'll [never] go away from you again as long as I live."[106] This theme became an understandable one in all of his letters. In another one, for example, he complained again about their separation--"Gripes! Honey, I love you and miss you so much that I don't know what to do. Sometimes I damned near go nuts. I never thought that I could miss anyone the way I miss you. You never really know till you get away from each other like we are now."[107] He always signed his letters, "Your loving husband, Dick."

A second readily apparent theme in his correspondence to Ann was, of course, how much he loved her. While on Sicily, his letters always included such testimony. Recall that V-Mail restricted his writing space much more than traditional stationary with its individual sheets of paper. In one V-Mail letter, in spite of the limited space, Dick penned some words that repeated themes he expanded on in other letters without restrictions on their length--"I love you more each day. I wish I could put my feelings towards you in words but there just aren't enough words available."[108] Three weeks later, just days before he left Sicily, Dick confessed again how much Ann meant to him--"I love you more each day. I never thought that anyone could mean so much to me. I sure found out. I think of you all the time & I think what a damned fool I was for not getting married sooner. I'll make up for it someday."[109]

Letters Dick received from home while in the ETO did not survive all of the movements of the 551st, from North Africa to southern Europe and, finally, to northern Europe. We know, however, that Dick's wife and mother sent him many letters. He impressed on both women how important these were to him. While in Sicily, one letter to Ann exudes the delight he felt on receiving correspondence-- "Whoope! The mail came in. Yep. It finally caught up with us. I got 32 letters of which 25 were from you. Boy, morale jumped sky high. Everyone got a pile of letters."[110] Dick stressed what such correspondence represented in another letter about a month later. The 551st had left Sicily and the mail did not reach them until they arrived at their next encampment near Rome. As Dick explained to Ann, "It finally got here, though, & I was one hell of a happy guy. You can't begin to imagine what mails means over here. It's the only connection I have to you & home. It seems funny that just pieces of paper & ink could bring you so close to me."[111]

Early in July, orders reached the 551st that it was to leave for Rome. So far, the battalion had not yet experienced combat in spite of its encampments in May and June at various locations "on the boot." Dick's feelings ("anxious to get into it") must have mirrored those of other jumpers as they heard of the fighting throughout the peninsula south of Rome. Because of timing, however, the battalion had just missed being involved in one of the most intense battle zones in the Italian campaign. When the 551st landed in Naples on May 23, 1944, the Army brass almost sent it to Anzio, about one hundred miles south of Rome on the western side of the peninsula. Although the Allies had landed there on January 22, 1944, they remained bogged down on the beach for the next four months. It appears that when the 551st docked at Naples on May 23rd, higher ups considered sending it up the coast to Anzio as reinforcement. However, the breakout from the beach occurred on that very day.[112] Because of this, the paratroopers were not sent to Anzio, or, for that matter, to any other engagement in Italy. Like the Allied units that moved north from Anzio to Rome, the 551st also headed to the city, but that happened in early July after Allies captured Rome on June 4, 1944. Areas around Rome served as the last training grounds for the 551st before it finally saw combat. The first combat operation the 551st participated in came in the summer of 1944. Historically, it was an important one, but one that has been relegated to a footnote in the history of the war in Europe--Operation Dragoon.

Chapter 4

On the Eve of Combat
"Almost into it"

After once again crossing the Straits of Messina, the boxcar trip up the boot to Rome took about two weeks. With heavy railroad traffic on the peninsula, the 551st's train often pulled off of the main track to a siding. When that happened, Dick estimates they sat there for sixty to ninety minutes. If they could, the troopers used that time to their advantage by bathing in the Mediterranean waters that touched the coastline, even though, as Dick points out, it was salt water. Dysentery plagued most of the men while on Sicily.[113] The condition did not disappear on the train ride north to Rome. During one of the sidings, the soldiers found themselves adjacent to a fig orchard. Tired of the C and K rations, Dick and the others ate the figs. They consumed a large quantity of the fruit. Once the men returned to the 40 and 8s, the lack of toilet facilities combined with the figs to create a major problem on the boxcars as the troopers experienced diarrhea. Dick explains that some of the men used their bayonet "to chop holes in the floor" that they used as makeshift toilets. Others "opened the doors and hung their behinds out." As Dick summarizes the journey north, it was quite a trip--"We fertilized the tracks all the way to Rome."

Once in the Eternal City, the 551st Parachute Infantry Battalion became attached to the Fifth Army as part of its Corps Reserve.[114] It had been almost three weeks since Dick had been able to write Ann.[115] When he could do so, his first letter from Rome could only tell his wife where he generally was--"I can't tell you where in Italy I am, but I will be able to later on."[116]

Lake Albano

How much later, Dick could only guess. For a brief time after they arrived in Rome, the battalion stayed at Lake Albano southeast of the Eternal City. Dick described the body of water in a letter to Ann-- "The lake was just a great big volcano crater that had filled up. It seemed as if you were way down in the earth when you looked around and you could look up at the rim of the crater."[117]

After the short stay at Lake Albano, the 551st set up camp about twenty miles southwest of Rome at Lido di Roma, a beach resort located near the Pope's summer home, the Castel Gondolfo.[118] The paratroopers bivouacked in a bombed-out former maritime college, the Collegio di 4 Novembre.[119] Dick recalls a model of a sailing ship in the courtyard. The troopers were thankful that regular food replaced C and K rations, and that they slept in a real bed instead of in their bedroll. While there, the soldiers received "quite a few passes to Rome."[120] Trucks regularly went from the camp into the Eternal City. Dick and his friends hitched a ride on one of them in order to get to Rome.

Decades later, looking back on those sightseeing trips, Dick realizes how lucky he was to be able to have that experience. A young man from a small town in New York would rarely have had such an

opportunity to see Rome. As he explains, "I was nineteen at the time, and looking back, I realize I was seeing things that ordinarily I would never have seen. I'm talking about the cathedrals, museums, the Forum, and the Colosseum, and things of that nature." Dick is honest to admit that he also frequented the bars in Rome, drinking wine and beer with other members of the 551st. As he concludes, "I

At The Colosseum; Dick is top row left

partied as much as anyone else." The visits to the Eternal City could be overnight ones. Dick recalls that the military made some private homes within Rome into "boarding houses." The families who lived in the residences put soldiers up for the night. When asked about how the Italians received the Americans, Dick replied that "the people treated us very well. They were hospitable, with no animosity." He remembers how hungry the local population was. Many begged soldiers for food. Dick stresses that he and others did not eat at the boarding houses. They frequented restaurants, although Dick recalls the menus as "very limited."

Dick visited the Red Cross headquarters in Rome during the last week of July. The Army unit that Ann's brother Charlie served in had reached the ETO. Dick wanted the organization to help him locate his brother-in-law's unit. He wanted to connect with Charlie, but that never happened. Another of Ann's brothers, Gus, was also in the Army. In a letter to his wife dated July 30, 1944, Dick voiced his hope that Gus would not see combat. As he wrote to Ann, he wished the war would be over before that happened.

While in the Lido di Roma, the 551st received word that its D-Day would be on August 15th.[121] The battalion was to be part of a massive invasion of southern France known first as Operation Anvil and later as Operation Dragoon. At the end of July 1943, the British Lieutenant General Sir Frederick Morgan brought up the idea of linking Allied "diversionary operations" on the Mediterranean coast of France to the much-discussed Allied invasion of northern France, code-named Operation Overlord. This became, in the conclusion of one prominent scholar, "the germ of Anvil-Dragoon."[122] Having read the British general's proposal, American Army Chief of Staff General George C. Marshall brought up Morgan's plan at the first Quebec Conference in August 1943. An obvious benefit of the proposal was that a military operation in southern France would deter the German High Command from sending reinforcements north to Normandy.[123] At the Cairo Conference in November 1943, strategists discussed the possibility of implementing Operation Anvil on the same day as the Normandy invasion.[124] One month later, at a December conference in Tehran, the Combined [American and British] Chiefs of Staff (CCS) gave its final approval to the Mediterranean operation.[125] From its beginning through its execution, one historian who has studied the invasion in depth points out that, "Anvil was never conceived as an operation in its own right. It was always considered subsidiary to the Normandy campaign..."[126]

The original plan called for American and British troops in Anvil to move north out of southern France after wresting the area from the Germans. When they did so, the veterans of Anvil would act as another arm in a classic pincer movement against the Nazis. As General Dwight D. Eisenhower, who commanded the Allied forces in the ETO explained in his World War II memoir, Allied troops moving north after Anvil "would protect and support the right flank" as forces that had landed at Normandy moved east toward Germany. If Anvil was not implemented, Eisenhower continued, "we would have to protect our right flank all the way from the base of the Brittany Peninsula to the most forward point of our attacking spearheads."[127] Aside from keeping the Germans bogged down in the Mediterranean area and eventually moving in conjunction with Eisenhower's right flank, Anvil would benefit the overall war in Europe in a third way. It would secure a second major port through which American troops could arrive in the ETO.

The port was Marseilles on the southern coast of France. For over two thousand years, it had been the leading harbor for the Mediterranean. With almost one million residents in the early 1940s, it was the third largest French city.[128]   If the D-Day landings at Normandy were successful, Cherbourg would be taken as a port of entry in northern France. As Allied troops broke out of Normandy and headed east, the Belgian city of Antwerp with its port would be another prize they would go after. But Eisenhower and Marshall wanted a southern European port of entry. None could equal Marseilles. In the United States, a "backlog" of newly trained infantry units awaited departure for the ETO. If they could dock in Marseilles, they would be used to support Eisenhower's right flank as it headed into Germany. Such an influx of men could not all be handled through "inadequate Channel ports or over the beaches of Normandy."[129] Operation Anvil thus offered three clear benefits for the overall Allied strategy in the ETO--it would occupy German forces in southern France so they could not be sent to Normandy as reinforcements, it would act as part of a pincer movement that protected Eisenhower's right flank, and it would secure Marseilles. One would think that the advantages of Anvil would have been obvious to the British as well as the American leaders who were supplying the vast majority of the troops for it. This, however, did not turn out to be the case.

Eisenhower identified his disagreement with English Prime Minister Winston Churchill over the efficacy of Anvil as, "one of the longest-sustained arguments I had with … Churchill throughout the period of the war."[130] The General saw the invasion of southern France by Allied forces as a military benefit for the overall war strategy. The Prime Minister, however, viewed that strategy not only in a military way, but also in a political vein. Looking toward a postwar world, Churchill feared the growth of Russian power in Eastern Europe. He wanted to send the additional Allied forces that were planned for Anvil into Italy and eventually the Balkans. In the Italian campaign, the troops could bolster Allied divisions that had been bogged down making their way "up the bloody boot." Forces used in Italy instead of southern France could hasten the Allies' arrival at Italy's northern-most border. From there, Allied forces could push through to the Balkans.[131] The English Prime Minister appealed his case to Roosevelt, but the president sided with his general, Eisenhower. On top of Churchill's opposition to Anvil, a military consideration made even its supporters pause on the simultaneous implementation of Operations Overlord and Anvil. All landing crafts (LCs) were needed for the Normandy operation. There simply were not enough LCs for both operations. In March 1944, the American Joint Chiefs of Staff called for the postponement of Anvil until mid-July.[132]

The success of Operation Overlord early in June 1944 led to the revival of its southern counterpart, Operation Anvil. The 551st, recall, had heard of the Normandy landings soon after it arrived in Sicily. Little did Dick and the other paratroopers know then that the D-Day they celebrated on that island would lead to the revival of an operation that would become their first combat mission in the ETO. Eisenhower brought Anvil back to life two weeks after the landings on the Normandy beaches. He recognized that it would be months before Antwerp could be taken from the Germans, while Marseilles could be a prize won that summer in Operation Anvil.[133] As Eisenhower argued on June 23rd, "Anvil opens up another gateway into France...The possession of such a gateway I consider vital."[134] In spite of Churchill's objections, the invasion of southern France was once again in the works. For security purposes, early in July the CCS ordered a new code name for the invasion. Supposedly, Churchill suggested "Dragoon" since he had been "dragooned," or coerced, into accepting the plan.[135] On August 5th, just ten days before Dragoon was to take place, the Prime Minister tried unsuccessfully to get Eisenhower to reconsider the invasion, arguing that the Allied divisions should be sent elsewhere. As Captain Harry C. Butcher, a Naval aide to Eisenhower, observed, "Ike said no, continued saying no all afternoon, and ended saying no in every form of the English language at his command."[136]

Chapter 5

Operation Dragoon
"Finally into it"

Eisenhower's staff set August 15, 1944 as the new D-Day for Operation Dragoon, ten weeks after Normandy's D-Day. As noted earlier, in mid-July while still at the Lido di Roma, the 551st received news that it would be part of the airborne arm of Dragoon. The announcement led to intense training throughout the rest of the month and the beginning of August. There were physical exercises as well as day and night speed marches with the soldiers wearing full combat gear. Over eight hundred paratroopers in the 551st battalion left the Lido di Roma at 2:00 A.M. on the morning of August 12, 1944. Dick wrote some letters home before his unit pulled out. In one dated August 12th, he again urged his mother not to be concerned over his safety. As Dick explained to Esther, "Say Mom, if you don't hear from me for awhile, don't worry cause I'll be pretty busy but I'll be alright so don't worry." Trucks carried the paratroopers to Montalto Airfield some ninety miles north of Rome.[137]

They had three days to prepare themselves for their first combat drop. The troopers arrived with a camouflage outfit that had been fashioned out of their regular jump suits. As Dick explains, the 551st did not receive outfits sewn from camouflage material. Instead, it made its own. Dick remembers how the men were ordered up on the roof of the college where they had been staying. Someone placed a cardboard box, with one side cut out for the head, over each soldier. The paratrooper stood there while another solider used a flit gun to spray green and black paint on the khaki-colored jump suit. After they arrived at Montalto Airfield, the troopers set up camp in what Dick described as "a marshaling area near the airport."[138] Just before its scheduled jump into southern France, Dick remembers how intently the 551st studied sandboxes with representations of the terrain the men would encounter once they landed. The sandboxes even held what Dick calls "fake buildings" and miniature trees to educate the jumpers on what they would see as they went into action. Additionally, officers used maps and aerial photography to familiarize the paratroopers with their target area.[139] During the day, soldiers could watch movies.[140] At night, some slept soundly while others fitfully, anticipating their first combat jump.

By the time the 551st was assigned to Operation Dragoon, Dick admits he was tired of the three months of training he and others had gone through since their arrival in the ETO. Dick felt no apprehension, only an eagerness to finally do

College rooftop at Lido de Roma
on way to Montalto Airfield

his part. He was able to begin that on August 15, 1944 as the 551st boarded forty-one C-47s for its role in Operation Dragoon.[141] Before getting onto the transport planes, the jumpers had one last mail call after which officers ordered them to destroy any envelopes they carried. If captured, such pieces of paper would give the enemy information that could identify them beyond the Army-issued dog tags each man wore.[142] The troopers helped each other apply green and black grease paint to their face and hands, creating a camouflage on their skin to match their jump suit. Some fifty years later, Dick's squad leader, Sergeant Joe Killgore, still remembered the weather on the 15th. Joe described it as "a very hot day."[143] The paratroopers boarding the planes carried approximately seventy-five to one

59

hundred pounds of equipment on them. Killgore saw it as "a load you wouldn't expect a decent jackass to carry."[144] Basic, of course, were the reserve parachute and the main parachute. Among the other items were hand grenades, an M-1 Garand rifle, ammunition clips, medical supplies, K rations, D candy bars, a canteen with water, packs of cigarettes and matches, carbine magazines, a pup tent, and a life preserver since they would fly over water.[145] Dick points out that such a listing is relative since some paratroopers might also carry equipment specific to their job, such as the radioman who packed a radio. The military command issued one last-minute item to the jumpers, a gas mask.[146] Concern arose that the chemical warfare Germany used in World War I might be employed again. The masks were cumbersome, and men tossed them as soon as they could. As Dick recalls, the mask was "the first thing we threw away," although he used the canvas bag it came in to carry other items. Dick remembers that he and his fellow troopers climbed aboard the transport planes sometime in the afternoon to fly about two hundred miles across the Mediterranean. As the 551st waited that day to enter history, Operation Dragoon had already begun earlier, at 8:00 A.M., H-Hour.

The invasion of southern France took place along a forty-five mile strip of the French coastline that bordered the Mediterranean Sea. The segment stood between two small resort villages, Cavalaire-sur-Mer and Agay. The month of August gave the military planners an advantageous weather-window. The days were warm with cool nights. In a letter to his mother dated August 12th, three days before Dragoon's D-Day, Dick shared his astonishment at the rain that fell outside of Rome this time of year. While the weather was clear when he wrote the letter, it had rained earlier in the day. As Dick observed, "They've got the biggest damned rain drops I ever saw. They feel like rocks hitting you. It doesn't take very long to get drenched." Heavy rainfall was not a problem, however, in southern France. The Allied soldiers landing on the beaches would not confront extreme tides or any swollen rivers as they made their way inland. The airborne component of Dragoon would not have to worry about any blasts of wind out of the Alps.[147] Rear Admiral Samuel Eliot Morison, a professional historian who wrote the official story of United States

Naval Operations in World War II, placed Operation Dragoon in the broad context of naval history. As Morison concluded, "it may stand as an example of an almost perfect amphibious operation from the point of view of training, timing, Army-Navy-Air Force cooperation, performance, and results."[148]

The landing forces in Dragoon were either American or French. The 3rd, 45th, and 36th United States Infantry Divisions composed the main force for the beach landings on August 15th. French divisions went ashore the next day. These first divisions equated to approximately sixty thousand men. Before Dragoon was over, at least seven more divisions were to take part in the invasion, bringing the troop commitment up to about two hundred and fifty thousand. The Allied Navy provided eight hundred and eighty ships to convoy the men and to provide gunfire support. (Sixty-five percent of those vessels were American, thirty-three percent British, and two percent French, Greek and Canadian.) Four thousand and fifty-six aircraft furnished aerial support, including the dropping of between nine and ten thousand airborne troops north of the Provencal Coast.[149] Then Lieutenant Colonel William P. Yarborough, who commanded one of the battalions in Dragoon, judged the role played by the parachute infantry units in the operation to be "the most successful Allied airborne assault of World War II."[150] Some previous drops in the ETO had proved disastrous, such as one in Oran and one in Sicily, but the one that accompanied Dragoon would be in a very different category.[151] Dick stresses that every parachute jump in an invasion learned from earlier ones. Dragoon's success reflected what airborne had learned in North Africa and Italy.

The American and British airborne units were brought together into what became known as the 1st Airborne Task Force (FABTF). Its code name was Rugby Force. A key job of the airborne arm of Dragoon was to block German attempts to send reinforcements to halt the Allied beach landings.[152] Dick points out that in addition to this mission, the paratroopers were to disrupt communication to the beach area by destroying transmission lines. To achieve these ends, the target area for the airborne drop was the town of Le Muy, about fifteen miles inland from the coast. Roads leading from the west, north, and east passed through Le Muy.[153] Because of this fact, if Rugby could take the town, German forces would be thwarted in any attempt to move toward the coast to stop the American troops coming ashore on D-Day. Three battalions, one regiment, and one brigade composed the Allied ten-thousand-man assault group.

In addition to the 551st Parachute Infantry Battalion, the other American units were the 550th Glider Infantry Battalion, the 509th Parachute Infantry Battalion, and the 517th Parachute Infantry Regiment. The British contributed the two-thousand-man 2nd Independent Parachute Brigade. Major General Robert T. Frederick commanded Rugby.[154] The men left in four hundred and forty-six C-47s from eleven different airfields in Italy.[155] Most of the ten-thousand-assault-group jumped from their planes in the early hours of Dragoon's D-Day, about four hours before the amphibious landings began. The 551st, however, dropped at the end of the day. Seventeen men from the 551st, though, became part of a one-hundred-man pathfinder group that jumped between 2:00-3:00 A.M. to reconnoiter the drop zone area. They also set up portable beacon signals to guide the main Rugby units that came in about one hour later.[156] The main body of Rugby Force thus landed under cover of the pre-dawn darkness. It had been standard procedure to do parachute drops in the dark so as to afford natural cover for the jumpers. In this way, it was much harder for enemy forces to target airborne troops as they floated down in the sky in the hours before dawn. Within Rugby, military planners chose the 551st for a special drop on August 15th. The battalion was even given a code name for its jump, Operation Canary.[157]

Because of the 6:00 P.M. hour, the 551st made airborne history by becoming the first daylight combat drop by United States forces in Europe.[158] On the flight from Montalto Airfield, Dick remembers looking down on the island of Corsica as the C-47s flew toward France. He had no idea he was part of a massive invasion of southern France, one he believes was surpassed in size and strength only by Normandy's Operation Overlord. The "big picture" (Operation Dragoon itself) had not been explained to the paratroopers. They had only been educated on their particular role in Rugby Force and then Operation Canary. Dick knew he was part of a bigger operation, but what that was, he did not know on August 15th.

Once the C-47s cleared the Mediterranean waters between Corsica and the French coast, the troopers knew that they were approaching their drop zone. As they had trained to do at Fort Benning and Camp Mackall, Dick and the other paratroopers watched for the sergeant's signal that it was almost time to exit the plane. It appears that Rugby Force jumped at altitudes much higher than was customary because of the elevated terrain in the DZ. Some members of the 551st recall exiting the planes from heights of 1,500 to 2,000 feet, although Dick has no such recollection.[159] He astutely points out that such citations should state whether the height was measured from sea level or from ground level. That could be a difference of hundreds of feet. Even amidst the noise of the airplane's engines, the jumpers listened for their orders to, "Stand up. Hook up. Sound off for equipment check." (Phrases, Dick points out, that are still used today as paratroopers exit an airplane.) After the men checked each other's equipment, each moved toward the door of the C-47. As Dick did so, he pulled his snap hook along the cable. The 2nd squad, 2nd platoon leader, Lieutenant Hecq, would be first out the door. Squad leader Killgore stood next to him. Dick, who served as first scout for the squad, waited next to Killgore.[160] Dick assumed the position taught him in training--feet first, head down, elbows in, knees bent, and hands grabbing onto the reserve chute. As he went through the door, the static line became taut, yanking the cover off of the main chute. Dick felt the force of the parachute as it opened. Killgore remembered seeing the air "full of lost equipment" as the force of the opening shock separated some items from the jumpers.[161] A pilot in an escort plane took a photograph of the historic daylight combat drop. Hundreds of descending parachutes are visible above the French countryside town of LaMotte, which stood very close to Le Muy.[162] Each chute carried a member of the 551st Parachute Infantry Battalion. The picture immortalized this jump, but Dick points out that captions which accompany the photograph seldom credit his battalion as being the one in the picture.

The Germans had created defenses against airborne forces. The enemy planted in the ground thousands of sharp stakes to impale a paratrooper as he landed. Americans nicknamed them "Rommel's asparagus," after German Field Marshal Erwin Rommel who was in charge of coastal defenses in France. The sticks measured twelve feet in height. Similarly, long poles placed into the ground were meant to wreck gliders carrying Allied soldiers and equipment. Additionally, the Germans stretched thick wires between trees to damage incoming gliders.[163] As the 551st descended, they landed in vineyards owned by the Valbourges Estate. Dick identifies it as "the Stevens Estate," since he understood that an Englishman, James Stevens, had married into the French family who owned the property. Some members of the 551st landed in trees, suspended above the ground by the parachute cords. Stevens and his wife Henriette ran from one tree to the next, trying to help the dangling troopers.[164] Dick knows of one member of the 551st, Gene Schmid of Company C, who landed in the vineyard. But Schmid did not end up on the ground or on the grapevines. Instead, he landed on one of the stakes used to hold up the vines.

Many were not as lucky as Dick who found himself squarely on the ground, in a vineyard adjacent to an open field. Immediately after cutting himself free of the parachute, Dick assembled his M-1 Garand rifle. As he explains, until he did that, he was "helpless" in enemy territory. When Dick separated himself from the chute, he cut out a panel to carry with him. He wrapped the piece around his waist.

Before they had taken off from the Montalto Airfield, members of the 551st had been given their assignment upon landing in their DZ. Dick explains that their immediate responsibility was to clear the area of the enemy to allow for the arrival of Waco gliders carrying more members of Rugby Force as well as heavy equipment. When the gliders began landing about fifteen minutes after the 551st had jumped, Dick describes the scene as one of "mayhem."[165] Over three hundred C-47s flew overhead. Each one towed two gliders that dangled side by side below the transport plane. The gliders were filled with 2, 250 members of the 550th Glider Infantry Battalion. They also carried jeeps and artillery. Chaos ensued as gliders cut loose of the C-47s that had brought them to this point. Cables that had tethered the gliders to the transport planes swung in the air, cutting off wings and fuselages. Planes, men, and equipment fell to the earth. Four hundred and four gliders had been involved in the invasion. Only forty-five remained in one piece. The FABTF suffered about one thousand casualties on August 15th, with about one-third of that number coming from the glider men of the 550th. Miraculously, the 551st lost only two men that day, with about five more seriously wounded.[166] Once the gliders landed, paratroopers in the 551st knew to head for an assembly area. Joerg, originally from Alabama, identified the spot by flying a Confederate flag he had brought on a tall pole.[167]

Dick recalls how the Stevens Estate "became a field hospital." The injured and wounded were taken inside of the house. One part of the residence served as the operating room; Dick believes it was the dining room. A chapel on the estate grounds functioned as a temporary morgue. Dick explains that the bodies of the dead were wrapped in parachutes and then stacked on top of each other until the graves registration detail could pick them up. One other vivid memory he carries with him of D-Day centers on the parachutes. Dick recounts how "women came out of the woodwork. They grabbed at the parachutes." Some chutes lay on the ground, some hung from trees. At first, the actions of the women puzzled him. Then Dick realized that they had been without material because of the war and the German occupation. Women took the silken chutes to use in making underwear and dresses.

In Operation Dragoon, Rugby Force experienced great success on its D-Day. Almost all ten thousand paratroopers landed in their target drop zone. Every C-47 plane returned safely to its base. The troops drove back German counterattacks.[168] Airborne forces easily took LaMotte.[169] They liberated Le Muy in the early afternoon. By the end of the day, the airborne arm of Dragoon had captured almost five hundred German soldiers as prisoners of war (POWs).[170] According to Dick, on the evening of the 15th the 551st "dug in for the night." While some members of the battalion slept inside of the main house, in the barn, and in outlying buildings of the Stevens Estate, others slept outdoors. In all probability, Dick stayed close to Killgore who recalled spending the night "in and around a sandy stream bed & ditch with a road block set up on a nearby road."[171] Aside from the fact that Dick acted as Killgore's first scout, the two men were friends. As Dick admits, "it was unusual for low ranking men to associate with higher ranking non coms, but he and I had a special relationship. We were very close friends."[172] The next day, August 16th, would be a critical one for the paratroopers as the battalion fought enemy forces in the German-occupied city of Draguignan.

The German LXII Corps, responsible for the defense of the Mediterranean coast in southern France, stationed its headquarters (HQ) in Draguignan.[173] On D-Day, the Germans had seven hundred and fifty soldiers in the city; as the day progressed, no reinforcements could be sent.[174] Dick remembers Draguignan's location to be about fifteen miles inland from the coastal town of Saint-Raphael. He emphasizes that Allied troops landing on the beaches faced German gun emplacements that the enemy controlled from its Corps HQ. Late on the night of the 16th, Lieutenant Colonel Joerg ordered his men to take the city. The colonel directed Companies A and B to lead as the

551st moved into Draguignan.[175] Dick obliquely identifies some "resistance" his unit, Company B, met as it carried out Joerg's orders. More to the point, as Dick and the rest of his company made their way down the streets, German snipers with rifles fired upon them as did German soldiers with machine guns.[176] The 551st took Draguignan the next day, the 17th. With a well-deserved sense of pride in his voice, Dick notes that even today a street named after the 551st remains among the roadways of the French city. In the process of securing Draguignan, Company A captured Major General Ludwig Bieringer, the District Commander. In so doing, the 551st made history in a second way, aside from its daylight combat jump two days earlier. Taking Bieringer as a prisoner constituted the first time Allied forces had captured a German general in Western Europe. One had surrendered in the North African campaign and another had been killed in action during Operation Overlord.[177] Casualties for the 551st grew that day from the few it had sustained on the 15th. In liberating Draguignan from the Germans, at least one more trooper died and about fifty were wounded.[178]

In a letter to Ann written nine months later, Dick summarized the events of August 15th and the following two weeks. As he announced to his wife, "The jump went off pretty good. We took Draguignan okay & captured a corps hq. with 2 generals and a whole mess of high ranking officers. We moved down to the beach & drove right along the shore. The old 551 did a lot of spearheading. We were the first ones in Cannes & Nice & some other small towns."[179] The brevity of Dick's summation belies the task before the 551st. On August 17th, after securing Draguignan, the Rugby forces met up with amphibious troops at various points inland from the Cote d'Azur, the Mediterranean coastline on the southeast corner of France. The battalion followed the Argens River as it flowed toward the coastal town of Frejus. On some days, temperatures reached one hundred degrees.

It took the 551st about a week to make its way south through the mountainous terrain to the Cote d'Azur. Known as the French Riviera, cities such as Cannes and Nice dot the coastal landscape.[180]

Dick and the 551st liberated both towns. German troops pulled out of Cannes, allowing the 551st and the 509th to take it without any exchanges with the enemy. But an event on a hill two miles outside of Cannes on the afternoon and night of August 21st holds a powerful memory for Dick. The Army knew it as Hill 105, a name taken from its height in meters. The Germans who fled Cannes fired upon Hill 105 using 280mm guns mounted on retractable rails near Nice, about fifteen miles from the hill. The 551st "bore the brunt of the counterattack."[181] Dick recalls it as "a terrible, terrible night." He believes the Germans killed between eighteen and twenty men from Company B. One friend was killed right next to him.[182] Dick and others in his unit carried members of Company B who had been killed off of the hill. Without body bags, they used shelter-halves. As Dick somberly explains, "it is something I sometimes still dream about."

Two positive events, the liberation of Cannes and Nice, followed that "terrible night" on Hill 105. On D+9, the 551st and the 509th moved towards the outskirts of Cannes as Germans withdrew. Allied forces entered the city on August 24th to the cheers of its residents who enthusiastically welcomed the troops.[183] Four days later, Dick typed a letter to Ann on American Red Cross paper, using what he called "a hinie typewriter." It was the first opportunity since D-Day to write her. Presuming the news of Operation Dragoon had made the newspapers back home, Dick acknowledged early in the one-page letter the role he had played. "I guess you've guessed," he wrote, "that I am now in southern France. I jumped on France on D day." That was the extent of his references to the war. Censorship, of course, would not have allowed a detailed account of his activities in the prior two weeks. Dick spent the rest of the letter telling Ann how much he missed her.

The very next day, August 29th, the 551st liberated Nice.[184] An Army staff photographer captured Dick's role in a public celebration of that event. He is prominent in a picture that appears in some books and articles on the 551st. Dick is seated on the back of a jeep, smiling. His right arm reaches out to grasp the hand of a resident of Nice who is obviously trying to thank the Americans for what they have done. The jubilation of the French people is apparent. In a letter to his mother a few weeks later, Dick tried to describe the scene he had witnessed in more than one French town. "You ought to see the people," he wrote Esther, "when we march through a town that we had just taken. The men, women, and children come out and mob you. In many cases we were the first Americans they had seen in four years."[185]   The   people were obviously grateful that   the   Germans   were gone.   The   French   had suffered   under   the occupation in more than one way. Dick referred to an   aspect   of   their economic   hardships when, in the same letter, he told his mother that,

"They hadn't seen white bread in 4 years." After the Americans gave the residents some, "They nearly went crazy."

In addition to the casualties it suffered in the first days of Dragoon, the taking of Cannes and Nice cost the lives of twenty additional soldiers in the 551st, and one hundred more were wounded. Overall, the battalion sustained a casualty rate of about 21% by the time it had helped to secure southern France.[186] Aside from major cities, the 551st helped to drive German forces from small villages inland from the Cote de Azur. On August 31st, the 551st and 509th moved eastward, toward France's border with Italy. Their mission was to protect the right flank of Allied invasion forces as they moved north from the beaches. In particular, Dick remembers the village of La Turbie, a town close to Monaco. The Germans held some fortified positions near it. The 551st occupied various locations on the roads leading to La Turbie. Once the two paratrooper battalions forced the enemy to move out, the Americans returned to Nice.[187]

The   success   of   Dick's   battalion   reflected   the   overall achievements of Operation Dragoon. Within two weeks of D-Day, Allied forces had liberated the major cities of Cannes, Nice, Toulon, and Marseilles. In the months to come, cargo records validated the importance Eisenhower's staff had placed upon the last city. By V-E Day, May 8, 1945, over four million long tons of cargo had arrived in Marseilles. That port also received most of over nine hundred thousand troops who arrived in Marseilles, Toulon, and Port de Bouc.[188] Dragoon's goal of occupying German forces in the south, to make it difficult for the enemy to send reinforcements to Normandy, also succeeded. Additionally, a month after Dragoon's D-Day, over one hundred thousand of the enemy had been taken as POWs.[189] Lastly, the plan to have military units in Dragoon link up with units from Overlord was first achieved on September 12, 1944 near Dijon, about one hundred and forty miles southeast of Paris. A squad from a French Corps that had taken Marseilles met up with a French armored division that had landed at Normandy.[190] The U.S. Seventh Army, whose three divisions had landed on the beaches of the Cote de Azur, would also move north over the next weeks to similarly hook up with Allied forces from Operation Overlord. Every goal that Dragoon had hoped to achieve had been met, and then some. One prominent historian reminds us that Dragoon occurred on what he calls "a flood tide of victory," ten weeks after Operation Overlord and two weeks after "the big breakthrough" in Normandy against German forces. Dragoon's greatest achievement "was to swell that tide by an entire Army group [the Seventh Army], which made the Allied advance into Germany irresistible."[191] Dick eventually became part of the Army's invasion of Germany. But first, he and the 551st fought enemy forces for three months in the Maritime Alps.

Chapter 6

In the Maritime Alps
"I'll be glad when this mess is over"

After its return to Nice from La Turbie, the 551st received a new assignment. German forces that had pulled out of the coastal and inland areas had moved into the Maritime Alps, a mountain range in the southwestern part of the Alps that extends to the Cote de Azur. The U. S. Seventh Army had begun moving north into France. To prevent attacks upon it from German troops now based in the Maritime Alps, paratroopers from the FABTF were moved into that region. The primary mission of the 509th, 550th, and the 551st was to protect the Army's right flank.[192] Dick emphasizes, though, that each airborne battalion functioned as an independent unit. Early in September 1944, the 551st received orders to move twenty-five miles north of the coast into the Maritime Alps.[193] Trucks carried them from Nice to Villars-sur-Var, a village on the Var River. At an elevation of about ten thousand feet, the 551st was to guard a thirty-five-mile-front. Company B, Dick's unit, was billeted in St. Martin-Vesubie.[194] Dick points out that his company sometimes based itself in other villages. For example, it also stayed in Puget-Theniers and Isola, but according to Dick, its longest stay was in St. Martin-Vesubie. In a letter written to Ann after the war had ended in the ETO, Dick summarized in two sentences what he did in a two and a half month period that began in early September and lasted until mid-November 1944--"We moved up into the Maritime Alps. We took such towns as Puget Theniers, St. Saveun, St. Martine Vesubie & others." He did not elaborate on what taking such villages meant.

Understandably, Dick did not detail his combat experiences in letters home to his wife or to his mother. It was the end result that he shared and took pride in, namely the liberation of villages in the Maritime Alps. French villagers expressed the same gratitude the French residents had displayed on the Cote de Azur.

Dick defines the mission of the 551st as one where the battalion patrolled the area and engaged German forces when they encountered them. He also adds, "We often sent patrols into Italy." The enemy had an advantage in the Maritime Alps because it chose a high elevation for itself before the Americans arrived. That allowed the Germans, in

Dick's words, to literally "look down upon the 551st." Their position allowed them to easily fire artillery rounds at the paratroopers. Dick was mystified then, and remains so today, as to how the Germans constructed the cement pillboxes up in the mountains. Some of them still stand today, as Dick can attest to after recent visits to the area. A professional student of the 551st describes Dick's battalion as one that "mounted a steady stream of heavily-armed and long-range infantry patrols into the mountains to prevent the enemy from launching any surprise attacks."[195] While on outpost duty, Dick reveals that he and others in his company, "watched for Germans in different passes through the mountains." Dick recalls staying in shepherds' huts when he drew the outpost duty. He could remain there for up to a week. In those months from September to November, Dick explains that his battalion "pushed the Germans back into northern Italy." He pointedly sums up the end result of the mission, "We tied them up."

Shepherd's hut

While in the Maritime Alps, the battalion still received and sent out mail to family back home, although it might be sporadic. In a long letter to Ann dated September 9, 1944, Dick mentioned that he had received a package from his mother that contained socks, nut bread, and photographs. He valued the pictures in particular. Dick asked his wife what had happened to some she promised to send. As he lamented to Ann, "I never have received them. Please try to send me a couple. You don't know what they mean to me." In this same letter, Dick returned to a theme evident in the correspondence he had written to his family since his arrival in the ETO. He again cautioned his wife, uselessly, not to worry. As Dick observed to Ann, "It just gives you gray hair & I like your hair just the way it is."

Some time passed before Dick wrote again to Ann, perhaps a month. Mail came in intermittently, and if sent out on a patrol, there was no opportunity to correspond. On October 6, 1944 he received five letters from Ann. Dick responded the very next day. He admitted, "I know it's been quite awhile since I wrote to you last, but I think you understand." The letter, written on a rainy day, gives several insights into Dick's life up in the Maritime Alps. He stated what was obvious to him, but perhaps not to his wife, "They really keep us going." As Dick shared with Ann, "I had just come in off a patrol & I hadn't shaved in a couple of days." Isolated up in the mountains, an ocean away from his bride of less than a year, Dick confessed that he still managed to hold her close to him, albeit in the form of a substitute. He asked Ann, "Do you know what I call the rifle I've got? 'Sugar Lips Ann.' I've got it carved in the stock." How tired Dick had become of their separation is apparent in the letter. "Boy, Honey, I'll be glad when this mess is over so I can get back home with you. I love you more each day. The days are plenty long over here but the nights are the worst."

Dick also appears to have gotten weary by this date of his time in France. He confessed this early in the October 7th letter-- "I'm dammed sick of France, though. It's been raining for the last 3 or 4 days now. The mountain tops are all covered with snow now & I guess it will be snowing in the valleys soon." When the 551st arrived in the Maritime Alps early in September, Dick notes that the paratroopers wore their summer uniform. The fall weather became cooler as the weeks went by. Still, "We were never resupplied." Once temperatures dropped, the airborne soldiers wore woolen olive drab shirts and heavy, woolen sweaters. Over that, the troopers clothed themselves in what Dick defines as "a fairly heavy jacket." Mittens warmed their hands to a degree. Members "bummed," using Dick's word, many of these pieces of cold-weather clothing from other military units, such as armored ones, whose members "took pity" on the paratroopers. Dick's childhood in Liberty, New York acclimated him to cold weather, but while in the Maritime Alps, the chill only added to the misery of the distance between him and Ann. Dick was tiring of the routine, the weather, and, above all else, the separation from his wife.

Between that October 7th letter to Ann and one he wrote his mother on October 22nd, Dick used a two-day pass to return to Nice where he enjoyed much warmer weather. While in St. Martin-

Vesubie, Dick sometimes received weekend passes. He hitched a ride down to the coast on one of the Army trucks that regularly drove into the town. Dick estimates he may have been given four or five of such passes in the two and a half months the 551st stayed in the Maritime Alps. The devastation from the war still struck him when he went back to Nice. He explained to Esther that Nice, "was a dammed ritzy city before the war." In spite of how it had changed, Dick wished his mother could experience the sights he had seen--"I wish you could see some of the places I've been." The boy from a small New York town had travelled far from home. Even though the war had marred Europe's landscape, Dick still felt in awe of what he had seen--the different worlds of North Africa, Italy, and now France. He wrote this letter to Esther after he reported back to his post in the Maritime Alps. As with his correspondence to Ann earlier in the month, Dick again addressed the frigid weather--"The nights are real cold & there is a lot of snow on the mountains. Yesterday, I was on one mountain & it snowed about 2 ½ inches in about 15 or 20 minutes." Liberty, New York probably could not have matched that rate of snowfall.

Dick in front row, second from left

On November 18, 1944, the 551st received orders to move out of the Maritime Alps. Dick explains that, "the Germans had pulled out" of the area. The 551st had not suffered heavy casualties while on the mountains, eleven killed and ninety wounded.[196] But recalling that the 551st entered combat on August 15, 1944 and remained in combat situations until the November 18th date, that three-month-period meant that the battalion ended up with the longest time in combat of any United States airborne unit in the ETO.[197] Dick cautions,

75

however, that being in the combat zone for that length of time did not mean that he and others "were firing their weapon every day." In any event, the record of the 551st qualified it for a much-needed R & R (rest and recreation). From the Maritime Alps, the troopers moved thirty miles south to the hills of Saint-Jeannet, a village near Antibes, a coastal town south of Nice. They stayed there for more than two weeks in pup tents. While the men underwent some training, it was light and they had time to themselves.[198] On December 7th and 8th, Dick and his battalion once again boarded the 40 and 8s that had carried them through Italy. Now, however, their destination was Laon, a French city four hundred miles to the northeast. Situated not far from the Belgian border, Laon also stood only thirty miles from Rheims, a French town that served as headquarters for the U.S. XVIII Airborne Corps. [199]

The troopers stayed at a cavalry garrison in Laon, with comfortable beds and warm meals. Dick describes his time there as one spent doing exactly what the military command expected the paratroopers to do, "relax." He does not recall anything in particular about his days in Laon, describing the city as "just a place to relax and unwind." While his men rested, airborne headquarters at Rheims called Joerg in to inform him that the 551st would be attached to the 82nd Airborne Division. It appears that the initial plan was for the 551st, after its R & R ended, to begin training on December 27th in preparation for its role in a spring movement across the Rhine River into Germany.[200]

As it turned out, the 551st's well-earned R & R in Laon lasted only about ten days. As Christmas neared, some of the men planned skits for a holiday show. Dick, who played a guitar, spent time preparing for his part in the production. The Christmas show never took place, however. The war changed dramatically for Allied forces in the northeastern ETO on December 16, 1944. On that date, the Germans began a massive counteroffensive in the Ardennes, a forest area that extends across France, Belgium, and Luxembourg. Germany's border lay just east of the Ardennes. Hitler, who personally planned the assault in a Belgian sector of the Ardennes, took the Allies by surprise. The encounter between German and Allied troops became known as the Battle of the Bulge. The 551st would join other units in an attempt to push the Germans back.

While the particulars were still unknown, news of what had happened in the Ardennes reached Laon on the first day of the enemy's attack. At approximately 10:30 P.M. on the 16th, Captain Jim Evans of Company B told his men that they would be moving out. It was not until almost twenty-four hours later, however, on the evening of the 17th, that 82nd Division HQ summoned Joerg. Originally, the 551st was ordered to Bastogne, Belguim to help hold that town's vital location as a road network. At 4:00 A.M. the next day, the 18th, Joerg informed his company commanders that Bastogne was their destination. But those orders were soon cancelled. Hours later a new set of instructions came down to Joerg. The 551st was to report to the commander of the 30th Infantry Division at Stavelot, Belgium. On the afternoon of December 19th, Dick and his fellow paratroopers climbed into Quartermaster trucks for the ride into Belgium. There they would join other units and participate in what one military historian, who himself was a company commander in the Battle of the Bulge, judged to be "the greatest battle ever fought by the United States Army."[201]

Chapter 7

The Battle of the Bulge
"It's pretty rough up here"

As detailed earlier, Dick had experienced combat twice before December 1944. For two weeks in August of that year, he fought in Operation Dragoon. Two and a half months in the Maritime Alps followed. During that time, from September to mid-November, an average of twenty-five artillery rounds fell daily on the 551st. On some days, the number reached one hundred and more as the paratroopers sought out and actively engaged the Germans in the mountainous areas that bordered France and Italy.[202] But none of the horrors of war Dick had seen in the summer and fall of 1944, not even Hill 105, prepared him for what he endured in the Ardennes. The Battle of the Bulge lasted for approximately six weeks. Over one million men fought in it, with Americans being some six hundred thousand of that number.[203] Casualties in the Ardennes surpassed anything Dick had seen during his time in southern France. At one rare point, on December 31, 1944, Dick was able to write to his wife and mother. Given the date, his thoughts might have been on other New Year's Eves. On this one, in 1944, he admitted to Ann, "It's pretty rough up here, but I'll make out." Of course, Dick downplayed the danger that surrounded him. Before his time was over in the Battle of the Bulge, he became a casualty. Additionally, he watched his 551st Parachute Infantry Battalion be so decimated in combat that the Army disbanded the unit just weeks after the Allies completely repelled the German's counteroffensive. Dick survived the Battle of the Bulge, but the 551st did not.

In December 1944, the Allied HQ based itself outside of Paris. Known as SHAEF (Supreme Headquarters, Allied Expeditionary Force), American General Dwight D. Eisenhower commanded the Allied forces in Europe. Eisenhower preferred to identify the six weeks from mid-December 1944 to the end of January 1945 as the Battle of the Ardennes, but the common name for it remains the Battle of the Bulge. The German's fifty-some-mile "bulge" in what had been the Allied line on December 15th became the source of the popular name.[204] Hitler's goals for the counteroffensive lay much deeper than merely an attempt to stop Allied movement into Germany. He hoped to divide American and British armies, retake Antwerp with its critical port, and perhaps even negotiate a peace in the West to free up his forces in the East. If the Nazis broke through the Belgian lowlands, they would position themselves between the United States and English armies. If the Germans reached the Meuse River west of the Bulge, they could then get to Antwerp, one hundred and twenty-five miles to the north. Diplomatically, even though the Americans and British shared a demand for Germany's unconditional surrender, Hitler dreamed that if his counteroffensive inflicted heavy casualties upon the Allies, one or both nations would negotiate an end to hostilities. That would free Germany to focus on its Eastern Front in the war with Russia.[205]

To accomplish all of this, German forces needed to seize at the outset two Belgian towns that possessed critical road junctions--St.Vith and Bastogne. Once in control of them, Hitler could move his troops in several directions. On the morning of December 16th when the counteroffensive began, St. Vith stood about twelve miles behind the Allies' front lines.[206] Two days later, enemy troops had penetrated fifteen miles into American lines. St. Vith fell, but Bastogne, further west, held as airborne forces moved in. As noted earlier, originally those troopers were to be members of the 82nd Airborne to which Dick's battalion had been attached. But as it turned out, the 101st Airborne Division went to the defense of Bastogne. If the orders Jorge had received back in Rheims had not been changed, at Bastogne Dick and the 551st would have been part of one of the most famous holding actions in the ETO. As it turned out, however, he and his battalion did not end up at Bastogne. Instead, they won a critical victory for the 82nd Airborne Division at the small village of Rochelinval, but one that became all but forgotten in the general history of the Battle of the Bulge.

Once the enormity of Hitler's counteroffensive became apparent to SHAEF, the 82nd and 101st Airborne Divisions were destined for the Ardennes. Both units belonged to General Matthew Ridgway's XVIII Airborne Corps. On December 16th, the 82nd and 101st constituted the only reserves SHAEF had. Both divisions had recently endured heavy combat in Holland. Before that, the 82nd and the 101st had played crucial roles in Operation Overlord, as well as the ensuing three-month-battle for Normandy. As with the 551st after Operation Dragoon and its months in the Maritime Alps, the 82nd and 101st were enjoying R & R near Rheims. The original plan had been that the two divisions would not return to full operational status until mid-January. But on December 17th, SHAEF knew it needed all possible reinforcements sent to the Ardennes. And that included the combat-weary, but also combat-proven, 82nd and 101st Airborne Divisions.[207]

Recall that the 551st was one of only two airborne battalions that held the status of an independent unit. That allowed the High Command to attach it to, and detach it from, other units as needed. Based on the presumption there would be future airborne operations, Dick's battalion became attached to the 82nd before Hitler began his counteroffensive. During the Battle of the Bulge, aside from the 551st Parachute Infantry Battalion, the 82nd Airborne Division consisted of three parachute regiments, a glider infantry regiment, two parachute field artillery battalions, an airborne engineer battalion, and an anti-aircraft automatic weapons battalion.[208] It is often falsely presumed that airborne troops fly or parachute into combat zones, yet Dick emphasizes that paratroopers are part of the infantry. As such, they move by ground transportation as well as by air. The 82nd began its "motor march" into Belgium on trucks just one hour after daylight on the morning of December 18, 1944. Because the 82nd had enjoyed a somewhat longer R & R than the 101st, and also due to the fact that it could be ready to move out more quickly, the 82nd left first for the

Ardennes. Dick and the 551st followed the next day, December 19th. He remembers very well the two-and-a-half-ton trucks that carried him and his battalion.[209] Known by the troops as "a deuce and a half," what Dick especially recalls about the ride is that fact that it was "so cold." The back of the truck had a canvas cover, but he points out that, "We were out in the elements, with no heater and with no overcoats." When asked how they slept during the two-day trip, Dick replied, "We tried to doze as much as we could, but it was a rough ride." At least for the men of the 551st, Dick remembers black soldiers as being their truck drivers.

The truck convoys that carried the two airborne divisions stretched for miles. Their progress proved slow. The vehicles rarely attained a speed of more than fifteen miles per hour over slick roads. Drivers continued the journey even during the night. Such driving proved especially dangerous on unknown roads because part of the headlights were covered to reduce the amount of light they emitted. The more illumination, the more readily the enemy could spot the convoys. After two days, as the trucks approached the front, traffic bogged down as the convoy met up with hundreds of refugees and soldiers moving west as the 82nd moved east.[210] General James Gavin headed the 82nd Airborne Division. He arrived in Spa, Belgium, the command post for the United States First Army, on the morning of December 18th after an all-night jeep ride from Rheims. At Spa, he received a new assignment for the 82nd. An elite German armored unit was approaching the village of Werbomont, southwest of Spa and ten miles west of St. Vith. Since the 82nd was en route to the Ardennes, Gavin was ordered to take command of the sector around Werbomont. The 101st would proceed to Bastogne. Gavin headquartered the 82nd Airborne Division in a farmhouse across a road from where his immediate superior, General Matthew Ridgway, established his HQ for the XVIII Airborne Corps. By December 20th, the day before the 551st arrived, the 82nd had created a semicircular defensive area around Werbomont that measured north to south about fourteen miles in width and east to west eight miles.[211]

The evacuation of St. Vith by the Americans on December 21st underlay the mission change of the 82nd. The Salm River ran directly west of St. Vith. The 82nd had to defend the Salm and keep communication open with American forces east of that river. The airborne troops thus set up a defensive line west of the Salm. The 551st played a key role in that defense. Once the entire battalion arrived in Werbomont, it was "unhooked from its two-week technical attachment to...the 82nd Airborne." The 551st then became part of the 30th Infantry Division to assist in the defense of the Werbomont sector. Dick and others in his battalion bivouacked in the small town of Ster, about five miles east of Werbomont. In the words of one scholar who studied the history of the 551st in-depth, this new assignment put the battalion "in an especially grim spot." It was situated between the towns of Stavelot and Trois Ponts; the Ambleve and Salm Rivers bordered the two communities. This was "where the very spearhead of the entire German thrust in the Ardennes was thrashing forward in the forest." Basic to the Allied response to Hitler's counteroffensive was the need to hold the shoulders of the Bulge, to make sure they did not widen. Some of Germany's best troops, the Sixth Panzer Army, tried to get through the northern flank of the Bulge, where the United States First Army held ground. The head of that German army ordered his crack troops--the 1st SS Panzer Division--to push through the northern end of the Bulge. If the Germans were successful in widening the Bulge at its northern end, they could reach the Meuse River at Liege and then be in Antwerp. The 551st was ordered to defend that "northern knob".[212]

When the 551st arrived in the Ardennes on December 21st, it found itself in just one small part of a dense, rough forest area that spread over two thousand square miles.[213] If the natural terrain by itself made the Ardennes less than inviting, the troopers lived everyday with harsh weather conditions. Cold winds, rain, mud, and snow only added to the difficulties Dick and other soldiers dealt with on a daily basis. With an average yearly rainfall of thirty-five to forty inches, the heaviest downpours come in November and December. Heavy mists accompany the rain; they can appear before noon and then return before evening. Snow can be a foot deep, more so in drifts.[214] These are just the general weather conditions in the Ardennes in December. The specifics could become more extreme, as Dick would find out. He remembers one incident that while amusing, speaks to how cold the temperatures could get. One day at mail call, a fellow trooper in the 551st received a package from home. It contained a box of small, orange marmalade jars. Dick recalls the brand name, "Your Heart's Delight." The marmalade was frozen.

When in the Maritime Alps, the clothing Dick wore did not furnish him with adequate protection against the harsh winter elements. Speaking for himself and the other men in the 551st, he explains that, "Most of the clothing we had were summer uniforms. Some had sweaters, jackets, [but] no overcoats." At one point while in the Ardennes, Dick acquired a pair of tank pants that insulated him more than the pants he had been wearing. The pants resembled a pair of overalls, including the suspenders. Like other Army-issued clothing, the tank pants were made from khaki-colored material. While the cloth was of a heavier weight than the pants Dick had been wearing, they were still not warm enough for the subzero temperatures. His footwear also failed to protect him from the winter conditions. Dick concludes that, "Our paratrooper boots were worthless since they were not waterproofed." Because of inadequate footwear, he points out that many men ended up with frostbite and frozen feet. Before he left the Ardennes, Dick became one of them.

In another place, such as Liberty, New York, the cold weather might have seemed perfect as Christmas Day drew near. In the midst of any battlefield in World War II, however, holidays could easily lose their special status. Keeping track of which day it was would not be a high priority for enlisted men. Just surviving the day, in a combat zone, was their focus. For the Allies in the Battle of the Bulge, an early Christmas gift arrived on December 23rd. Hitler had chosen the opening date of his December 16th counteroffensive to coincide with weather conditions that made it impossible for the Allies to mount aerial attacks on German ground forces. That changed on the 23rd when the cloud cover and fog lifted. Dick holds a memory of that weather change--some rays of sun allowed him to see his shadow. Over three thousand Allied planes attacked enemy ground forces and dropped supplies to isolated American soldiers, such as those at Bastogne. The skies stayed clear for four more days.[215]

Left to right: Al, Dick, Archie

At Dick's childhood home in Liberty, one can guess what the 1944 holiday season meant for Esther Field. She had three sons, and all three served in the Army during the war. Allen entered the military in August 1942, Arch, Jr. in March 1943, and Dick in May 1943.[216] In the front window of her home on Mill Street, Esther hung a Service Flag, also known as a Service Banner, in their honor. The custom originated in World War I as American families announced to the world how many of their members served in the military. With a wide, red border on all four sides of a rectangular cloth, the middle of the banner was white with a blue star, or stars, in its center. One star represented one member of the family who wore a uniform. Some flags were handmade, others purchased. Dick's younger sister, Carol, is still alive. She was ten years old when the United States entered World War II in December 1941. Thus as a child, she lived with her mother when Dick and his two brothers served in the military. Carol has some clear memories of the Home Front. She distinctly remembers that a Service Flag hung in Esther's window. It had three blue stars, one for Allen, one for Arch, Jr., and one for Dick. Carol believes her mother bought the flag.

She also reaffirms what is obvious about Esther's state of mind during the war. According to Carol, Esther "worried constantly" about her sons. Two of them saw combat in the ETO, Arch, Jr. in an armored unit and Dick in airborne. Allen basically stayed stateside. One out of every three G.I.s during World War II never went overseas. The service of the three Field brothers reflects this statistic.[217] For those that did leave the United States, most soldiers were not combat infantrymen. Instead, they served in support capacities, such as field artillery, headquarters, and the Quartermaster Corps. Yet front lines could become blurred, as cooks and supply officers found out during the Battle of the Bulge. While the exact definition of a "combat soldier" can be debated, regardless of how narrow or broad one makes it, such soldiers were a minority of those who served in the United States Army.[218]

When Dick was in paratrooper training back in the States for his combat role, Esther tried to locate on a map the various camps where the Army sent Dick. Late in 1943, she became frustrated when she could not find Camp Mackall. Dick wrote his mother a letter in which he tried to help her by identifying large towns near it.[219] Realize that the holiday season was approaching when Esther wrote that letter sharing her disappointment in failing to locate the camp. It would be the first Christmas that her sons would not be able to be with her. Carol recalls how her mother left the Christmas tree up for several weeks after December 25th. Esther had expected that Dick would come home on leave that month. When he did not, she postponed taking the tree down. She hoped he still would show up one day soon after Christmas.[220]

If Dick's mother was like millions of others on the Home Front, she listened to President Roosevelt when he spoke to Americans on the radio. Carol believes the two of them would have done so on the evening of December 24, 1944 when the president delivered his Christmas Eve message. Broadcasted from the Roosevelt family estate at Hyde Park, New York, one sentence in particular held relevancy for the Fields. The President promised families that "the Christmas spirit lives tonight in the bitter cold of the front lines in Europe and in the heat of the jungles and swamps of Burma and the Pacific islands."[221] Because of the different time zones, it was already Christmas Day in the ETO. But the Field family in Liberty had no idea Dick was in the Ardennes, a battle that by Christmas was well-covered in American newspapers. Accounts referred to the 82nd Airborne Division, yet Dick's parents, wife, and sister had no idea that the 551st had been attached to it. For all they knew, he was still in southern France. The Fields would have had no way of knowing that the 551st left that area of Europe in mid-November, or that his battalion ended up in the Bulge about a month later.

As with the days, the nights of December 24th and 25th were cold ones in the Ardennes. The cloud cover that had cleared the day before Christmas Eve meant that the temperature dropped below zero. Snow fell. With great effort, soldiers moved and rubbed their hands and feet to keep them from freezing. As noted earlier, the 551st had the standard issue summer uniform, although some of the troopers had added sweaters and jackets to it from their months in the Maritime Alps. But the Army never officially re-supplied the battalion. Dick remembers holding his canteen inside of his jacket to keep the water from turning into ice. In a V-Mail letter to his wife written six days after Christmas, Dick shared his hope that she had "a nice Xmas." He then told her about his meal on December 25th --"I ate K rations myself & was glad to get them." Some soldiers fared much better than Dick in respect to their Christmas dinner. One enlisted man in the 26th Infantry Division, dug in just northeast of where Dick was, enjoyed "turkey and the trimmings." General George Patton wanted his men in the Third Army to eat a similar meal. Most received it in the form of hot turkey sandwiches with gravy. At Bastogne, where the Germans surrounded troopers in the 101st Airborne Division, most of the soldiers ate unheated white beans with a cold broth that had thickened. One infantryman several miles west of where the 551st encamped ate a C ration can of pork and beans along with a fruit cocktail can that had come in a package from home.[222] The latter item made his Christmas meal somewhat more festive than what Dick ate. It could be that Dick's holiday meal resembled that of many others, if not most, of those enlisted men who spent the holiday in the midst of the Battle of the Bulge. On December 25th, the 551st encamped in Ster, almost five miles east of Werbomont. In the afternoon on Christmas Day, Joerg received orders from the XVIII Airborne Corps to head to Rahier, a place Dick defines as "a small collection of houses" about midway between Werbomont and Ster. There the 551st once again became attached to the 82nd Airborne Division.[223]

Gavin, as Division Commander, chose the 551st for a special, nighttime mission that was to take place on the evening of December 27th. The general wanted to assess if the time was right for the Allies to begin a counteroffensive against the Germans on the northern shoulder of the Bulge. He needed information on the location and strength of enemy forces. The goal of the raid was to capture some Germans from whom such intelligence information could be taken. In order to be back before dawn, the 82nd unit sent in would only have about six hours to make its way through first Allied lines and then into German lines. Once in enemy-controlled territory, the Americans would capture some Germans to bring back as POWs. Perhaps influencing Gavin's choice of the 551st was Joerg's personal reputation for courage and the fact that the battalion had not yet been "bloodied" in the Battle of the Bulge as had other units in the division.[224] Dick emphasizes, too, that as an independent battalion, the 551st could move out more quickly than larger units. Being "small and mobile" meant, in Dick's characterization, that the High Command assigned the 551st "a lot of grunt work."

Dick's memories of his first combat assignment in the Ardennes are vivid ones. Gavin's orders specified that the 551st was to take its prisoners from a German Command Post at Noirefontaine, about four miles southwest of Rahier. Dick defines Noirefontaine as "not really a village. It was really a big farm or estate." The battalion left Rahier around 9 P.M. on the 27th and encountered the 508th troopers about two miles and two hours later, midway through the trek.[225] It was, in Dick's memory, "pitch black." He emphasizes that "there was no front line" as the men moved. The situation was, in his words, "chaotic," with "German and American troops all over the place." The paratroopers eventually reached a road that a map indicated would get them to the estate. The attack began before midnight. Joerg had ordered Company B, Dick's unit, to lead. It would be followed by Companies C and A.[226] Army intelligence officers had cautioned Joerg before the battalion left Rahier to watch for mines on the road. The pathway also lost its appeal when the soldiers found that the freezing weather had turned it into solid ice.

Dick explains that to facilitate their movement on the road, to avoid any mines that may have been there, and to give them what he calls "a little better cover," Company B decided to walk on the left-hand shoulder of the road. After making it about half to two-thirds of the way down the road on the shoulder, the Germans saw them and fired machine guns at the troopers. The machine gun was on the same side of the road as was Company B. Company B quickly "dove into a ditch" on the left-hand side of the pathway. Trooper Charlie Brubaker from West Virginia ended up lying right next to Dick in the ditch. Charlie wanted to jump across the road when there was a lull in the enemy's firing. His plan was to move up a ditch on the right-hand side of the road in order to come up on the machine gun's flank. But

when he rose up and put himself on the icy pathway, he slipped. The Germans proceeded to fire upon Charlie who made a very visible target in his Army uniform set against the

Dick in Noirefontaine today; ditch on right

white ice. Dick and the other paratroopers, as well as the Germans, believed Charlie was dead after a shower of machine gun fire descended upon the road where he lay. Suddenly though, Dick heard

Charlie's voice--"I'm coming back." Charlie jumped into the ditch, landing right on top of Dick. Miraculously, his wounds were not serious. Dick realized how lucky his unit was. The enemy fired "slightly to our left. If the machine gun had been set up to our right, the Germans would have wiped us all out by being able to fire right down the ditch."

As it turned out, the ditch gave them cover so that the company could, as Dick explains, "inch our way forward." With grenades, the troopers "wiped the machine gun out." A horse and wagon, Dick recalls, suddenly bolted out of an archway attached to the building complex that the Germans used as their Command Post. The wagon held perhaps six or seven enemy soldiers who were trying to run away. Members of Company B purposely fired at the horse, killing it, to halt the attempted escape. The wagon overturned. Troopers shot the two or three Germans who tried to run away on foot and took the others as prisoners. They then set the Command Post building on fire with phosphorous

Picture Dick took of Command Post today

grenades and rounded up some prisoners. Other members of Company B, who had been held back in the initial assault, covered the battalion's withdrawal. Because of its leadership in the attack and in protecting the withdrawal, Company B suffered the worst casualties that night. The 551st lost four men and another fifteen were wounded.[227] All were from Company B. The return trip to Rahier proved even more "tricky," to use Dick's word. The captured enemy POWs posed a potential problem when the 551st made its way back from Noirefontaine through first German and then American lines. If any of the prisoners alerted their fellow Germans as the troopers moved stealthily through the pre-dawn hours, the 551st would again have to engage enemy fire. But in the end, the battalion returned to Rahier without further incidents.

Dick rightly concludes that "the raid was very successful." Gavin had wanted at least one prisoner. The 551st returned with around twenty-five.[228] For about a week after Noirefontaine, Dick and his unit had a respite from further combat. The 551st remained at Rahier where it had been sent right before the raid. With the ground covered in ice, the men did the best they could to dig foxholes in the earth. Some members of the battalion dug in on a hillside south of Rahier known as Haute Bodeux, located behind Basse Bodeux.[229] At one point during those days, someone probably told Dick and others in the 551st that there would be an opportunity to send some letters home. That is when, on December 31st, Dick wrote to Esther and Ann. In his mother's letter, Dick opened with an apology and an explanation--"I guess you've been plenty worried about me & I'm sorry that I haven't written sooner, but I've been pretty busy." He was able to tell her his general location. "I'm in Belgium now and it's quite rough but there isn't anything to worry about." Dick made similar statements to Ann. He cautioned both women that his "letters will probably be few and far between" because he knew he would not have much time to write in the immediate future.

Chapter 8

The Allied Counteroffensive
"I have never seen such hell before"

With what the High Command believed to be sufficient intelligence information, it set a January 3rd date for the beginning of a counteroffensive against the Germans. The basic plan was to push the enemy back through the bulge in the Allied line as it stood on December 16th. The VII Corps, with two armored divisions and two infantry divisions, would advance from the west to the east. Ridgeway's XVIII Airborne Corps was to move forward in a southeasterly direction to protect the VII Corps' northern flank. The only division within the Airborne Corps that would attack the enemy would be the 82nd.[230]

As division commander, Gavin came up with an assault plan built around what appeared to be "a huge stable door." Its hinge would be located at Trois Ponts in the east, a hamlet the Germans controlled. Fifteen miles wide, the door would swing south to east until it met the Salm River. Located in the very center of the bulge, the Salm ran north-south, making it a river the enemy had to cross before they could get back to Germany. The job of the paratroopers would be to close that stable door, forcing the enemy to return east and retreat back to its homeland. Gavin planned to lead with three parachute infantry regiments--the 517th (to which the 551st had been attached for the counteroffensive), the 505th, and the 325th.[231] Dick's battalion was to be, in the words of its historian, "a connecting tissue between regiments."[232] Each regiment received orders as to the towns or villages it was to move the Germans out of. One author characterizes those assaults collectively as "a series of brutal frontal attacks in some of the worst winter conditions in the last fifty years."[233] And as Dick emphasizes, they were to do so without sufficient artillery or armored support.

For the 551st, its first assignment was to retake the ridge of Herispehe and the village of Dairomont, both located south of Trois Ponts and west of the Salm. To do this on January 3rd, the first day of the Allied counteroffensive, Dick's battalion had to move one and a half miles into what was then German territory. They crossed a sunken road at Basse Bodeux. With no cover, and the enemy dug in on high ground, the 551st suffered heavy casualties. Still, it moved south toward its objectives. After crossing an open field, the 551st confronted a steep, lengthy ridge that was part of the Herispehe wood. Fir trees gave the Germans on the ridge a perfect defensive position. Intense enemy artillery, mortar, and machine gun fire inflicted heavy casualties on the 551st. One commentator used words such as "annihilation" and "slaughter" to describe the losses. In spite of this, Dick's battalion moved further south toward its objective of Dairomont. By nightfall, the 551st reached another wooded area, the Hamba Woods. That put the troopers in position to attack Dairomont the next day. [234] But their battalion commander, Colonel Joerg, questioned the wisdom of mounting the assault. In the first day of the counteroffensive, casualties from the 551st equaled almost one-third of the battalion. In more human terms, dead and wounded totaled one hundred and eighty-nine. That loss rate was exceptional for the first day of the counteroffensive. Joerg contacted the 517th and asked that his battalion be relieved. His request was denied. In the words of those around him, "Joerg was stunned. He could see what was coming."[235] With more assaults ordered across open fields against Germans on higher ground, the colonel worried about how his weakened battalion could mount successful attacks. The weather only added to his concerns and to his casualties.

The ground was frozen the night of January 3rd. But in one respect, that did not matter. The 551st troopers had no intention of digging a foxhole in which to sleep. When the counteroffensive began, the Americans had to deal with an overcast sky, fog, and snow that measured two feet in depth. In temperatures that dropped below zero, they had moved up, and then down, hillsides filled with trees where snow drifts were twelve to fifteen feet deep. The troopers wore inadequate clothing, and the boots that they took such pride in provided no protection against the wet earth.[236] Dick explains that men feared freezing to death if they slept in a horizontal position on the ground. Instead, many tried to get some rest leaning against a tree or sitting at its base. One soldier Dick knew, Johnny Castellano, must have thought he would be safe if he sat on the ground to catch some sleep. He did so, holding his rifle. Unfortunately, Johnny still became frozen in that position, with his weapon attached to him. He did not die, but Dick watched as soldiers carried him to an aid station, his rifle seemingly glued to his body. Others were not so lucky. At least twenty-four members of the 551st died of acute hypothermia during the first days of the counteroffensive.[237]

On the second day of the Allied counteroffensive, Joerg moved his men further south to carry out Gavin's orders to take Dairomont. Germans controlled the hamlet. Because Dick's company had not sustained the casualty rate of the others, Joerg chose Company B to lead the attack. Dick explains that at first he and the other troopers moved through a "heavily wooded area" that offered them cover. But once they left it, to move into "open land where farmers grazed animals," the landscape gave the Germans an easy target. In Dick's words, the men were "like ducks on a pond," all too visible as targets for someone with a rifle. He remembers mostly "small arms fire" raining down on the 551st. Company B ran into a hail of intense sniper fire as it moved through snow that went up to the men's knees. Joerg sent in Company A. It dispatched two squads to put some German machine gun nests out of commission. One moved to encircle the enemy while the other moved forward toward it. A lieutenant who led the latter squad, Dick Durkee, saw that his men could not fire directly into the nests without perhaps hitting troopers from the other squad who were moving toward the Germans from behind. Durkee decided to give an order not usually heard in the European Theater. The lieutenant shouted that they were to fix their bayonets onto the end of their rifles. Screaming loudly, Durkee and his squad lunged at the enemy soldiers. Dick recalls his company being adjacent to Company A. The men in Company B thus hear the screams, but at the time Dick and the other troopers did not know the noise was part of the bayonet charge. Durkee thus led a

highly unusual but successful attack that seized the area from the Germans with a heavy enemy casualty count.[238] More than once in recent years, Dick has visited a memorial to the 551st that today sits in a field outside of Dairomont; its inscription mentions the bayonet charge.

As it turned out, the 551st took Dairomont two times. Joerg thought his men had secured it on January 4th shortly before 10:00 A.M., but a barrage of German artillery fire forced Dick's company to pull out, moving back into the protection of the woods. The battalion spent the night in and around the small village. The next day, January 5th, began on what might have appeared to be some positive notes. The sun, which had not been seen for well over a week, came out. The clear sky allowed Allied airplanes to again mount attacks upon the German forces, although by midday the fog had returned. Company B retook Dairomont that morning. But the battalion was still contending with enemy fire. An aid station was set up at Dairomont to deal with casualties; Dick takes note of this fact in sharing his story because, medically, he visited it two days later. By the end of January 5th, the progress of the Allied counteroffensive as a whole still

Dick at Dairomont Memorial today

looked especially grim from the perspective of the 551st. Its original battalion strength had been decreased by fifty percent, down to just three hundred and twenty-five men. The cost of moving about two miles into German-held territory had been high. When one realizes that those few miles had taken over two and a half days, the price becomes even more prohibitive. Once the 551st held Dairomont, Dick's company walked across a low level of the Salm River, directly west of the village they had just taken. But German fire forced them to return to Dairomont.[239]

The next day, January 6th, saw two major decisions that affected the 551st. In the afternoon it was detached from the 517th regiment. During its time with this unit, Dick's battalion had participated in most of the intense fighting in the sector assigned to the 517th. There might have been a brief hope by Joerg's staff that the new attachment to the 504th would result in a momentary respite for the men.[240] That was not, however, to be the case. In fact, an order received on the 6th by Joerg from the 504th signaled just the opposite. There would be no rest for the 551st. Unbeknownst to enlisted men such as Dick, on January 6th the 551st was defending the left flank of the entire 82nd sector.[241] Instead of staying at Dairomont, the regimental commander ordered the 551st to move about one mile east and capture Rochelinval, a town on the Salm River. In the wake of the Allied counteroffensive begun four days earlier, the Germans were retreating eastward. Rochelinval gave the enemy what one writer judges as its only opportunity in that area "for a safe retreat over the Salm." Put another way, the town was "the last German bridgehead on the Salm in the 82nd Airborne's sector."[242] After mounting brutal attacks over the course of the last four days against other enemy-held Belgian villages, Rochelinval became the new assignment for the 551st.

Knowing what his men had endured already, Joerg voiced his concerns to Colonel Reuben Tucker, commander of the 504th. Looking back, one can see four factors that collectively account for Joerg's reluctance to attack Rochelinval. First, the battalion was considerably below strength. Altogether, the 551st now consisted of two-hundred and fifty men, down from the approximate eight hundred that had arrived in the Ardennes about two weeks before. Dick's Company B numbered only eighty-three. The 551st was attacking a position where the Germans had an estimated five hundred soldiers.[243] Second, the physical condition of his men caused Joerg concern. Of those still on the line, many suffered from frostbite.[244] Food allotments had been running low, so the caloric intake had declined. The troopers were tired both from what they had endured over the last few days and also from a lack of adequate provisions. One item they had in large quantity, Dick dryly notes, was water since it surrounded them in the form of snow. But they did run low on food. Dick recalls that on more than one day during the counteroffensive he went without a meal. Even when he and others ate, Dick points out that the C rations were "stone cold" and the K rations dry. Dick's recollections about the food support Joerg's demand that he wanted his men fed before they began the attack on Rochelinval.[245]

A third factor that weighed on Joerg concerned the terrain his battalion had to move across, and then climb, to reach Rochelinval. It favored defenders of the village, not those attacking. Rochelinval stood on a high bluff. Below it, at a distance of about two to three hundred yards, was a forest of pine trees. The trees would give the troopers cover, but after they came out of the forest, a large piece of flat land would lay before them. The Americans had to cross this open pastureland. Once they did so, the soldiers would slip downward into a steep gully. One author likens the gully to a moat, with ice-coated snow inside of it. From the gully, the troopers would confront a steep slope that ascended to a bluff. So it would be down the gully, across the moat, up the slope, and onto the bluff. At its top, some members of the 551st would face one last hurdle. A rock wall stood above the gully, with almost a dozen German machine guns along it. The wall did not run the length of the entire bluff, but it would have to be surmounted by some of the troopers. Enemy artillery and mortar units added to the firepower that the 551st would encounter. [246]

As if all of the above considerations were not sufficient to move Joerg to question his orders, one fourth factor influenced him. Joerg could not get the 504th command to promise adequate artillery or armored support. Why this was denied to the 551st is not clear. Unquestionably, communication between the battalion and the regimental HQ was poor due to equipment and weather conditions.

The most prominent historian of the 551st has concluded that "bad luck" by itself, however, cannot explain, "the ungodly series of SNAFUs" that plagued the 551st. That writer finds fault with both Colonel Tucker and General Gavin. Additionally, the "orphan" status of the battalion itself might have been a factor. It could have acted as an unconscious influence in explaining the failure of the High Command to support the 551st's assault with artillery and armor. A historian of the battalion cites a human tendency that he calls the "neglect of the orphan." Put another way, in Dick's words, Joerg's men might have seemed almost "expendable" by the 504th.[247]

Because of all of these considerations, on the night of January 6th Joerg asked that the orders received by the 551st to attack Rochelinval be withdrawn. He either wanted the attack postponed or he wanted reinforcements. Joerg saw it as suicidal for his battalion to go forward and attack Rochelinval in its present strength. He felt so strongly about this that he appealed directly to General Gavin.[248] In spite of Joerg's protestations, the orders remained. The 551st was to attack Rochelinval the next morning. Joerg's general concern for his men had already endeared him to the troopers. His appeals on January 6th simply gave more evidence of that concern. Dick reflects the loyalty the men felt for their commander--"We really loved that man. I know of no one in the battalion who spoke ill of him. He was highly respected." While Joerg and some of the officers under him recognized their orders amounted to a suicide mission, Dick did not. As such, he was representative of other troopers. They did not understand "the big picture" of what they would confront the next day. If they had known, they would have been as unsettled as was Joerg.

The assault against Rochelinval began around 6:00 A.M. on January 7, 1945. Joerg ordered Company A to lead the attack from the left. Coming out of the woods, Dick's Company B came in from the right. Company C, lowest in strength, was temporarily kept in reserve at the top of a hill in the woods.[249] As noted earlier, only about two to three hundred yards stood between the trees and the gully. The Germans withheld their fire upon the approaching Americans until the paratroopers reached about the midway point in the open field between the woods and the gully. When they did, the Germans fired artillery, mortar rounds, and machine guns at the troopers. By 8:30 A.M., Company A was "almost eliminated as a fighting force."[250] Unknown to the men in the open field at that time, the leader they so revered, Lieutenant Colonel Wood Joerg, had been mortally wounded around 8:00 A.M., about the same time enemy fire was decimating Company A. Joerg had been monitoring the progress of the attack from the woods. Shrapnel from a German artillery round penetrated his helmet. As Company A suffered heavy casualties, and Joerg lay dying, Dick's unit continued to move toward Rochelinval despite the barrage of enemy fire. Before long, Company C joined the fray. A powerful memory Dick has of the move across the flat piece of land is how "the field was strewn with bodies, both the dead and the wounded." He also recalls "constant small arms fire" being directed at the troopers. Those who made it through the open field went down the gully, across the "moat," and up the bluff. Eventually, what was left of the 551st reached the top of the bluff. As it turned out, only Company A confronted the rock wall; Companies B and C reached the top of the bluff in areas that had no wall. All companies, however, became involved in hand-to-hand-combat once they arrived at the village. Around noon, one lone American tank arrived and was enlisted in the assault. The fighting ended around 3:00 P.M. with the 551st, or what was left of it, in control of Rochelinval. [251]

For Dick's battalion, the attack on Rochelinval signaled the end of the battalion's formal participation in the Battle of the Bulge. At the close of the day, there simply were not enough men left to reconstitute the unit as a battalion. When the Allied counteroffensive began on January 3, 1945, the 551st numbered six hundred and forty-three men. On January 8th, one day after taking Rochelinval, only one hundred and ten remained. In assaults mounted by the 551st in the Ardennes, such as those at Noirefontaine, Dairomont, and Rochelinval, it suffered a casualty rate of eighty-four percent. Among parachute infantry battalions, only the 509th ended up with a higher rate.[252] Four and a half months after the assault on Rochelinval, Dick wrote a letter to Ann. Because the Germans had surrendered and censorship was no longer imposed, he could write more freely than he had of what happened in the Ardennes. Dick summarized in several sentences what he had seen--"I was on the First Army front. We pushed the Krauts back to the Salm River...The 551 caught hell. There were 8 men left in A Company, about 12 in B Company and all the other companies were just as bad off. The rest of the men were either killed or wounded...I have never seen such hell before & I hope I never have to again."[253]

The most detailed chronicler of the 551st Parachute Infantry Battalion characterizes its role in the January 1945 counteroffensive as the "tip" of "the spearhead" for Airborne forces on the northern shoulder of the Bulge.[254] Its critical presence in the battle in the Ardennes has been lost, however, in general histories. Even in those of the 82nd Airborne Division, Dick's battalion is slighted since the 551st was what its own members called "a bastard battalion." It clearly "belonged" to no one regiment, division, or corps. Its strength resided in the fact that as an independent battalion, it could be attached and detached to larger units based on military considerations. Undoubtedly, at times this led to a feeling among other airborne units that the 551st was not one of them. The camaraderie among the paratroopers of the 551st remained somewhat insular. It existed between the men themselves, but since HQ attached and then detached it several times during the war, the brotherhood did not go further than the battalion itself. This is not to say that members of the 551st did not feel some identification with units they were assigned to, most prominently the 82nd. But the bonding combat soldiers experience remained primarily within the 551st battalion. After the Battle of the Bulge ended, and credit was given to the 82nd for the prominent role it played in the German pushback, troopers in the 551st had every right to ask, "But what about us? What about the accomplishments of the 551st?"

Two days after Dick's battalion took Rochelinval, the High Command temporarily relieved from further assignments three of the divisions within the First Army that had suffered the most casualties. The 82nd Airborne was one of them. It still included the survivors of the 551st, a little over one hundred of them, recall. Automobiles drove

Dick's fellow troopers to Juslenville, a village near Rochelinval. Belgian families took them in, giving the troopers a much-needed rest.[255] Dick, however, was not one of them. He had pulled back from his climb up the bluff below Rochelinval to help a wounded comrade. In getting his buddy to an aid station, Dick might have also unintentionally saved himself from being one of the last casualties of the 551st as it took the village.

Chaper 9

A Serious Case of Frostbite
"My dogs froze"

As members of Company B climbed the bluff below Rochelinval, enemy fire fell around them. A mortar round exploded near one of Dick's friends, Marshall Clay, a full-blooded Navajo Indian from Arizona. The two paratroopers had gone through Fort Benning's jump school at the same time. From that point on, as Dick puts it, "We stayed together," since both were assigned to the 551st. At Rochelinval, when Dick estimates they were "part-way up the bluff," pieces of "metal, dirt, and rock" hit his friend from the impact of the mortar round. One side of Marshall's face, in particular, was torn up. "He was a mess," Dick continues in remembering the scene. "He was full of blood." Marshall "could not see." When Dick saw what had happened to his friend, he stopped the climb and went to help. Due to the seriousness of Marshall's condition, to leave him where he had fallen would have proved fatal. In Dick's estimation, his buddy would have either bled or froze to death. With no medic in sight, Dick crawled, "half-dragging" Marshall, over the same open field it had taken hours for the 551st to cross. (Due to enemy fire, it was impossible to walk upright across the field.) In fact, Dick was in such a hurry to save Marshall that he dropped his own musette bag on the ground. He left it on the bluff, filled with personal items such as his driver's license, Social Security card, and photographs.

Once back in the cover of the woods from which the battalion had emerged hours before, Dick still could not find a medic. Marshall, blinded by his wounds, could not see. With his friend's arm draped around Dick's neck to support most of Marshall's weight,   Dick managed to get them both to the regimental aid station in Dairomont. The Army had converted the village's schoolhouse into an aid station. Space inside of the building was therefore limited, in spite of the heavy casualties experienced that day. The medical staff found a bed for Marshall, but Joerg, mortally wounded, lay outside.[256] With his friend now safe, Dick went over to the pot belly stove that warmed

Dick & photo of aid station

the building. He took off his paratrooper boots and socks. Dick placed them in front of the heat that emanated from the stove, intending to dry them before he returned to join his company. He remembers that the part of the socks the toes slipped into was stiff. Dick placed his exposed feet close to the heat. A doctor passed by. The physician saw not only Dick's "dogs" (a slang word for "feet"), but also the ice crystals between the toes. In fact, Dick admits that the end of his toes had turned black. In a cursory exam, the doctor poked the toes with an instrument. He then delivered an order that sixty-seven years later, Dick still remembers the precise wording of--"You're out of here."

That medical order began a two month reprieve from the war for Dick. He first went to a field hospital in Liege, Belgium for a brief stay. From there, an Army ambulance took him across Belgium and into France. Because of letters Dick sent to his mother and wife in January 1945, we can trace some of his movements that month. He wrote both women V-Mail on the 12th. Very similar in content, Dick told Esther and Ann at the very beginning of the letters that he was "back in France," in a hospital. He immediately followed that announcement by explaining that he was not wounded. As Dick continued, "I just froze my feet & got trench feet, too. I won't lose any toes, so don't worry about me." He further detailed how this had happened--"I went 4 days with wet feet in the snow & zero weather. The old dogs refused to operate any further." Twelve days later, on January 24th, Dick wrote another V-Mail to his mother. By that date, the Army had transferred him to a hospital in England. The format of the letter dictated brevity. Dick used most of the space to confess to Esther that he was "a little homesick." The progress of the war gave him hope, however, that the end of the conflict might be in sight. Some criticism crept into even that positive note, though--"I only pray that this mess gets over with soon because I'm thoroughly disgusted with the whole dammed thing."

An Army physical examination form that Dick has a copy of states that "frozen feet" accounted for his two-month stay with the 91st General Hospital in England.[257] The core group of Army medical personnel who comprised the staff had arrived in April 1944. The 91st operated out of a British medical installation known as "Churchill Hospital," located near Oxford. While the hospital buildings were the property of the British government, funds donated from the United States underwrote much of the construction. American doctors, nurses, and technicians volunteered to work at Churchill Hospital before the United States officially entered World War II. They treated the English population beginning in the fall of 1940 when the Germans started to bomb London and other English cities. Once the Japanese attack at Pearl Harbor brought America into the war, the British turned Churchill Hospital over to the United States Army. The 91st General Hospital stood four miles from the center of Oxford. The city is the site of Oxford University, one of the leading institutions of higher education in the world. In a letter to Ann written months later, Dick identified the location of the English medical facility by pointing out that he had been at a hospital "where the big college is."[258] As it turned out, Dick arrived at the 91st General Hospital just a few weeks after the number of patients it served reached a high of 1,681.[259]

He would not have been alone in the reason for his hospitalization. Up to half the soldiers in Army hospitals had not suffered any wounds. In December 1944, in addition to the 78,000 combat casualties, the Army counted another 56,000 soldiers as non-battle casualties. Most of the first number was from the Battle of the Bulge and most of the second was due to trench foot. Numbers were even higher in January. As one Army historian concluded, "Trench foot put far more men out of action in the Bulge than the Germans did."[260] (Today, Dick refers to his foot problem as "frostbite" to distinguish it from "trench foot," a condition he associates with feet that become immersed in water. Yet even Dick used the phrase "trench foot" in his January 12, 1945 letters to his wife and mother.)

Dick's recovery from frostbite took time. He spent weeks in bed and had to go through rehabilitation. Dick recognizes he was lucky to not have lost any of his toes. His condition was discovered in time to save them because he had taken Marshall Clay to the aid station in Dairomont. The freezing temperatures that Dick experienced in the Ardennes cut off the circulation in his extremities. The skin in his feet decayed, especially around his toes. The tissues under the skin became black and hard as, Dick explains, capillary vessels were destroyed by the subzero temperatures. While at the 91st General Hospital, Dick was often in pain. He recalls his treatment as one where he exposed his bare feet to the air, with "cotton between the toes" to separate them. A roll of towels under his feet raised them up. The greatest concern was gangrene; he probably received the new antibiotic drug penicillin to guard against that. Early in Dick's stay, when he was bed-ridden, medical protocol dictated that he use a bedpan. But he preferred a toilet, so one night Dick crawled on his hands and knees to reach a bathroom. A nurse found him on his way to his goal and, with amusement, furnished him with a wheelchair for the rest of the journey.

Once Dick could walk, he traveled to Oxford and enjoyed the sights the city offered. On such trips, the soldiers were required to wear their cartridge belt, with their rain coat folded in the back of it, and their helmet. Double-deck buses from the hospital carried patients into the university town. About halfway between those two points, the bus stopped at a pub. Dick recalls some of the patients stayed there and others continued into Oxford. Dick emphasizes how grateful the British people were to the American soldiers. Small trucks stood on street corners offering coffee and donuts. "We could not buy anything. The English people insisted on paying." In Oxford, he recalls visiting a dance hall that he believes the USO ran. It offered live music, girls to dance with, and sing-a-longs. Dick especially listened for two of his wartime favorites, Vera Lynn singing "We'll Meet Again" and "Lili Marlene." Back at the hospital, women in the British Red Cross regularly visited, bringing coffee and donuts.

Chapter 10

With the 505th Parachute Infantry Regiment
"There is no more 551st"

By the end of February 1945, Dick had left the 91st General Hospital. On February 28th he wrote a V-Mail to Ann from France. He brought his wife's attention to a new APO return address on the envelope, "As you can see, I've moved again. I'm heading back up now. I don't know how long I'll be getting there." Clearly, Dick understood he would be joining an infantry unit, but he was not sure how long it would take for him to hook up with it. When he left England, he had hoped he would return to the 551st. His orders, however, were to report as a replacement to the 505th Parachute Infantry Regiment that was part of the 82nd Airborne Division. At one point during the Battle of the Bulge, the 551st had been attached to the 505th. In that same February 28th letter to Ann, Dick vented some of his frustration at how the Army operated, "We have to put up with a bunch of crap in these dammed replacement pools, but it will be over soon (I hope)." As he had for several months, Dick counted on the war ending in the immediate future. He found out at a French train station that the Army had no choice but to send him to a new unit. The 551st had been deactivated. While standing at the station, Dick "looked down the platform" and saw Sergeant Tom Thornton, who had been in his old battalion. Thornton had been the highest ranking noncom in Company B. When Dick asked the sergeant if he was headed back to the old battalion, Thornton announced, "Field, there is no more 551st."

Unknown to Dick, the Army disbanded his battalion during his stay at the 91st General Hospital. On January 27, 1945, Gavin spoke to the one hundred and so survivors of the 551st at a theater in Juslenville. They had been resting there, recall, since their assault at Rochelinval. The general explained that their unit would be deactivated as a battalion and soon be disbanded. The surviving paratroopers would be reassigned to units within the 82nd Airborne Division. One day after this meeting, the Allies pushed the Germans back behind their own border; the enemy now stood where it had six weeks earlier when Hitler began the counteroffensive. Officially, there was no longer a "bulge" in the Allied line. Even this news--the official ending of the Battle of the Bulge--did not serve as a reason for celebration among those from the 551st. Their battalion was no more. In the touching words of one trooper, "A piece of paper did something the Germans couldn't do—eliminate our gallant battalion."[261] At full strength, the 551st should have numbered a little over eight hundred men, but after the Bulge, they had lost about seven hundred troopers. Most casualties came from the wounded and the dead, but a small number were missing in action and prisoners of war. What Joerg had judged to be a suicide mission--the assault on Rochelinval--only added the final blow to the battalion. The Army would have had to inject hundreds of replacements into the 551st to bring it back up to a number approaching full strength. That was not a realistic option.

Some members of the battalion felt that other considerations could have been in play early in 1945 that also account for the disbandment. They heard that Ridgway disliked the idea of independent paratrooper units, and he had wanted to disband them even before the Ardennes. Other survivors vented their anger at Gavin, who they believed was embarrassed at the casualties the 551st suffered in the Ardennes, especially at Rochelinval where Joerg had asked for a postponement of the attack.[262] If the battalion "disappeared," the casualties it suffered could not easily come back to haunt Gavin's own record as its commander. But these were just theories that allowed the survivors of the 551st to focus their bitterness at two tangible targets, Ridgway and Gavin. Dick probably summed up the basic reason for the disbandment of the 551st in a letter he wrote to Ann. He explained its dissolution by noting the obvious fact, "…there wasn't anything left of it."[263]

At the train station in France, when Dick heard of the disbandment, "it was a blow," to use his own words. He explains that "being a small unit, we were like a family." That feeling did not transfer to the 505th Parachute Infantry Regiment when he joined it at Camp Suippes, located in northeastern France near the city of Rheims. Dick appears to have arrived in Suippes sometime late in February or early in March 1945. The 82nd Airborne Division returned to that camp over a two-day period beginning on February 20th. Replacements for the division's three regiments--the 505th, the 507th, and the 508th--began showing up then. Some had been members of the 509th and the 551st. The Army had disbanded both independent battalions; like the 551st, the 509th had sustained heavy casualties in the Battle of the Bulge.[264]

Dick wrote Ann a letter on the 24th of March. In it, he shared with her the news of his assignment to the 505th. One can detect ambivalence in his comments. Dick is proud of the 505th, but at the same time he feels as if he is back to "square one." As he wrote to his wife, "I'm in a new outfit & I expect to be with it from now on. It's a good outfit, too. It's kind of hard to get used to it, though, because I have to make friends & get to know new officers and noncoms. It's almost like coming into the Army again. I'm getting along fine, though." At least Dick remained in an airborne unit. Four such divisions existed in the ETO--the 13th, the 17th, the 82nd, and the 101st. One had not seen combat (the 13th), and one had only recently been in combat with the Battle of the Bulge (the 17th). Of the four airborne divisions, the 82nd had the deepest roots in American military history. The Army had first activated it in World War I. Dubbed the "All-American Division" because the soldiers in it hailed from all forty-eight states, the unit spent more consecutive days on the front line than any other division from the United States. Dick likes to point out that the famous World War I soldier Sergeant Alvin York, a recipient of the Medal of Honor, was a member of the 82nd. Deactivated after the war, the military activated it again in February 1942. Within the division, Dick's assignment to the 505th was a point of pride for him. The unit had an enviable history among the other parachute regiments. It was the only such airborne unit to make four combat jumps in World War II--Sicily, Salerno, Normandy, and Holland.[265] Within the 505th regiment, Dick served in the 1st Battalion, Company C.[266]

In March, the first month that Dick was with the 505th, the 82nd practiced some training jumps at an airfield close to Camp Suippes. Although he did not understand it at the time, those were rehearsals for what the High Command code-named Operation Eclipse, an airborne drop into the German capital city of Berlin. After taking off from the airfield, Dick recalls the DZ as "a plowed field." The soft ground buffeted their landings. He never forgot one of those jumps because of an accident that befell another paratrooper. That man's main parachute did not open. Instead, Dick and others on the ground watched when a "streamer" developed as the trooper descended through the sky. Paratroopers use that word to describe what the visual effect is as the parachute becomes a long, nylon train descending to the earth instead of a billowing chute. Dick remembers he and others on the ground shouted, "Pull the reserve [chute], pull the reserve." The jumper eventually did that, but at what Dick estimates was about fifty feet from the ground. Because of that short distance, the soldier "hit the ground hard," as Dick describes the landing. The man was not seriously injured. As such, he was ordered to immediately board another plane and do the jump again.

In April 1945, Dick's second month with the 505th, his unit became part of a movement to surround enemy soldiers in the Ruhr area of Germany directly east of the Rhine River. Allied actions at the end of March by British General Bernard Montgomery and American General George S. Patton resulted in some 350,000 German troops encircled in the area. In what has been called the "Ruhr Mop-Up" and the "Ruhr Encirclement," the Allies proceeded to squeeze the Germans into a pocket on the eastern side of the Rhine near Dusseldorf. It became known as the Ruhr Pocket. The river ran near its western border. The German cities of Dusseldorf and Cologne, both on the Rhine, stood close to the northern and southern extremities of the pocket. On March 30th, Gavin received orders that the 82nd Airborne Division was to defend a section along the Rhine centered at Cologne, just north of Bonn. With the 101st Airborne Division, the 82nd closed the western side of the Ruhr Pocket along a south-north line that followed the Rhine River. Part of the 82nd's assignment was also offensive; it was to make contact with enemy forces across the river to assess German strength there.[267] It appears that units aside from Dick's participated in such missions since he has no recollection of his unit crossing the Rhine.

Dick and the 82nd left Camp Suippes on April 2, 1945. The division traveled by truck and train. Two days later it reached the area assigned to it along the Rhine. Dick remembers seeing Cologne from the back of a deuce-and-a-half. He describes it as "a city in ruins, flattened" as a result of the Allied bombing campaign. One sight in particular "amazed" Dick, as he puts it. The cathedral appeared "relatively unharmed." Gavin placed his infantry regiments next to the river, with the 505th in the most southern position. The 82nd sent out patrols on that first night, the evening of April 4th - 5th. They moved across the Rhine and some made contact with the Germans, fulfilling the orders the division had received. The assignment on the border of the Ruhr Pocket proved not to be a difficult one. Dick characterizes it as "almost like an R & R," with only "light combat." Most of the troopers did not bivouac in the field. Officers allowed them to stay in abandoned homes. Dick billeted with others in a mansion located on the Rhine. Rumor had it that the house belonged to a German doctor attached to an enemy military unit stationed right across the river from the mansion. Whether that was true or not, it seemed to explain why German artillery never targeted the home. Dick recalls a motorcycle that the absentee owner left in the garage. The men were allowed to ride it at their pleasure. Unknown to Dick and others in the division, the 82nd was being held as strategic reserves, hence its light duty and comfortable living environment.[268]

Immediately after his arrival in the Cologne area, noncoms distributed mail to the troopers. Dick received two letters from Ann, both dated March 13, 1945. They had taken less than three weeks to reach him, which led him to conclude, "So that wasn't too bad on the mail service." Dick replied the same day, April 5th, from, as he wrote at the top of the letter, "Somewhere in Germany." Up until that point, Dick told Ann that it had been awhile since he received any correspondence from home--"My mail hasn't been coming through very good because of moving around so much, but I guess it will start catching up quite soon now." From this comment, he appears to be hoping that his unit might stay along the Rhine for awhile. The weather was pleasant, with the temperature rising. Dick enjoyed the scenery. He observed to Ann, "This is a pretty country. You wonder how it is that so much evil can come out of such a pretty country." As in his earlier letters, Dick shared his desire to come home. "Gosh Honey, I miss you so dammed much. When I think of all the good times we've had together, my heart gets sick with dread for the rest of the time I'll have to spend over here. God, I hope it won't be too long."

If geographical progress toward Berlin was any indicator, it would not "be too long" before the war in Europe ended. Allied forces had already crossed the Rhine River early in March at a small town, Remagen, south of Bonn. That put American and British forces only three hundred miles from Berlin. Now, more than a month later, the 82nd confronted a German resistance that was weakening in the Ruhr Pocket. Most of the enemy forces in the pocket surrendered during the month of April, but not without Allied and German engagements. On April 15th, in the words of one historian, Dick's division found itself "pinched out of the fight by friendly units moving up the east side of the Rhine from the south." At that point, the 82nd received a new assignment for approximately six hundred and fifty square miles in its sector. Among other duties, the division was now to help occupation authorities with searches, arrest German military deserters, and round up armaments.[269] The 505th went to Bruhl, a small town near Bonn. The unit continued patrols in the area.[270] In some of the small villages, Dick recalls enemy sniper fire that targeted his unit.

One prominent historian concludes the following about the events that Dick was now a part of--"In the final stage of the western war, the Anglo-American armies advanced in the face of sporadic and ill-coordinated opposition. As always, the infantry bore most of the pain of clearing pockets of resistance."[271] Statistics show that the war in the ETO proved just as deadly for American forces in April 1945 as it had in June 1944, the month and year of the famous invasion on the beaches of Normandy. In April 1945, over ten thousand Americans were killed; that number was fifteen hundred more than those who had died in February 1945.[272] Dick's life was certainly still in danger, although it might not have appeared that way. He readily admits to feeling what he identifies as "trepidation" when his unit moved out to engage the enemy. Dick knew how close the war was to ending, and like other soldiers, he did not want to be among the last casualties. In a letter to Ann at the end of May, Dick summarized the activities in his prior month with the following few sentences: "We moved up to the Rhine River, right on the Ruhr pocket. We sent patrols across the river & when the pocket was cleared, we moved on up near the Elbe River."[273] The assault crossing of that waterway would be the next assignment for the 82nd Airborne Division.

Dick's regiment was the first one to move out of the area near Cologne for the Elbe. Colonel William Ekman commanded the 505th. On April 26, 1945, members of the 1st and 2nd battalions boarded 40 and 8 boxcars. By train, they traveled more than two hundred miles to a staging area close to Bleckede, Germany, on the western side of the Elbe. The town was located at an unusual point along the river. The Elbe made a U-shaped turn at Bleckede, with the open part facing east. Before dawn on April 29th, the 1st battalion (Dick's unit) and the 2nd battalion reached Bleckede. The troopers marched into town around 4:00 A.M. and took up residence in some abandoned houses. It was then that officers shared the details of their mission with the enlisted men. What they heard gave them pause. Concern arose again that after all they had been through, they could become a casualty just as the end of the war seemed near. As noted earlier, Dick shared this fear. But orders were orders. Ridgway wanted the troopers from the 505th to cross the Elbe on the night of April 29th, the very day the 1st and 2nd battalions had arrived in Bleckede. The regiment was to secure a bridgehead at the eastern side of the Elbe, after which combat engineers would erect bridges across the river.[274]

Snow began to fall right before 1:00 A.M. on April 30th, the designated hour for the crossing to begin. At that time, the only troops available to mount the assault were still the 1st and 2nd battalions of the 505th. They would form the first wave to cross the Elbe. The rest of the 82nd Airborne units would arrive later. Engineers identified four sites for the crossing that would establish four different beachheads on the eastern side of the Elbe. Orders called for the 1st battalion to cross at the base of the "U" and at a southern site. The 2nd battalion would cross at two northern sites. Within Dick's 1st battalion, Companies A and C (his company) would lead the assault. As it turned out, his unit landed far ahead of the 2nd battalion. When the latter arrived at its two northern debarkation points, it did not find any boats there, so the 2nd ended up crossing almost two hours after the 1st battalion had done so.[275]

The one-thousand-foot width of the river between the western and eastern sides at Bleckede should have taken about thirty minutes to cross. The 1st battalion's navigation of that distance, however, proved neither easy nor quick. Those two factors explain why Dick "vividly remembers" the crossing. A large amount of guns from six artillery battalions provided cover for the boats as they made their way to the enemy's side of the Elbe. As Dick explains, the shelling was meant "to soften up the other side of the river." Unfortunately, some of the shells fell short of their target, landing near the boats carrying Company C. Less than a month later, Dick wrote his wife about the incident--"We were lucky that night. We had a bunch of artillery short rounds (our own artillery) land right among us." Another incident prolonged the crossing time. According to Dick, the current carried the boats up onto what he calls "an island in the middle of the river." That "island" was really a sandbar. His unit thought it had reached the far shore. The men got out of the boats, spread out, and prepared to attack German positions. The troopers then discovered that they were only about half-way across the Elbe. They had to re-group and return to the boats. Dick and the others then had to drag the small crafts to the other side of the sandbar. By 3:00 A.M., all four companies from the 1st and 2nd battalions had crossed the river. Two and a half hours later, the engineers began building the first Allied bridge across the Elbe. The paratroopers encountered little resistance from the enemy. The 82nd accepted surrenders from German units.[276]

An intelligence officer in the XVIII Airborne Corps concluded that the attack by the 505th regiment the morning of April 30th "broke the crust, the outer defenses" of the enemy. A historian of the 82nd Airborne judged it to have been "a high-risk operation with little time to prepare [for it]." Casualties for all of the 82nd Division regiments involved in the crossing of the Elbe numbered twenty-one killed, one hundred and twenty-two wounded, and eleven missing-in-actions.[277] The 82nd's crossing of the river coincided with one other significant casualty, Hitler's suicide on April 30th in Berlin. In a letter Dick wrote to Ann that detailed his movements during the war, he explained that after crossing the Elbe, "We took a lot of prisoners. We took a bunch of small towns. At this time the Reich was breaking down. Then it came. The Armistice."[278] Dick referred to, of course, the formal surrender by Germany to Allied forces. German representatives of the Nazi government signed the document at Rheims on May 7, 1945. It became effective the next day, May 8th. The 82nd Airborne at that time was bivouacked at Ludwigslust, a German town near the Baltic Sea, about twenty-five miles from the Elbe River.[279] Dick remembers it as a farming community.

In two letters to his wife, Dick shared with her how his unit acted upon receiving the news that the war in the ETO was finally over. As he wrote, "I thought when that day came that everyone would be running around drunk & raising hell. But it wasn't that way at all. Everyone just acted natural." Even Dick, who like all of the other troopers had anticipated the news, did not celebrate in any special way. He explained to Ann what one could call "a downside" to the enemy's surrender. "I'm not as happy about it as I thought I would be. You're still just as far away as ever. I wonder if I will get home now or have to take a crack at the Japs first. I'm sweating it out." As Dick correctly surmised, SHAEF had, for the moment, decided to send the 82nd and the 101st to the Pacific where they would participate in the invasion of the Japanese homeland. Until such a time, the two airborne divisions served as occupation troops within Germany.[280] About two weeks after what became known as V-E Day (Victory in Europe Day), Dick described to Ann what he had been doing. "Since then, we've been moving all over this sector, policing towns, guarding prisoners, and things like that."[281]

Chapter 11

Waiting to Go Home
"Sweating it out"

In May 1945, approximately 144,000 enemy POWs passed through the lines of the 82nd Airborne Division as German military units surrendered. Some did so as a result of the Allied encirclement at the Ruhr Pocket and others as the Allies advanced across the Elbe. After V-E Day, the numbers grew even more. For the rest of May and the first week of June, the division sorted the enemy soldiers into groups relating to their rank and unit. Once the POWs were sent to enclosures, troopers guarded them. The 505th controlled camps around the towns of Dellien and Zeetze, near Ludwigslust.[282] Dick recalls those weeks when his unit guarded what he remembers as "thousands" of German POWs. The Allies housed them in what Dick describes as "big fenced areas with tents." The surrounding farm country stabled horses. Dick patrolled the stockades riding one of them. Even while doing this, his thoughts had to be of home and family. In more than one letter to his wife and mother, Dick referred to "sweating it out," meaning, he was waiting to come home. What he wanted desperately to avoid was being sent to the Pacific Theater. But the proximity of a certain waterway in the Middle East, an easy route for such a transfer, could prove his undoing. As he observed to his mother, "That dammed Suez Canal is awful convenient." If he were to stay in the ETO, Dick estimated a four to eight month stay.[283]

The first of those months saw the 82nd move from Germany into France. On June 2, 1945 the division left Ludwigslust for Camp Chicago, located close to Laon, France. It took three days to make the trip by boxcars and trucks. While in Laon, Dick did what so many American soldiers did, he mailed a package home of "souvenirs" he had picked up in the course of the war. He sent the box to Ann, apparently in a hurry because he did not put in a detailed description of the contents. A long letter to her dated June 17, 1945 took care of that omission. The inventory of the items sent speaks to what American soldiers typically picked up in combat zones and to what Dick's personal interests were. Like other GIs, he sent home enemy weaponry--a wooden-handled knife "from a Kraut paratrooper," a German bayonet "picked" from when he had crossed the Elbe, and a dagger Dick "took off an SS troop colonel," inscribed in German with the phrase, "All is for Germany." He also enclosed some German medals and watches.

While scavenging such items from battlefields is as old of a custom as war itself, other objects Dick sent home reflect his sense of history in that he saved memorabilia related to his time in the ETO. Three of the objects were associated with Dick's airborne service. One was a small American flag worn on his arm when he jumped into southern France, and another was his "jump jacket," worn throughout Operation Dragoon. Dick identified the third one as "the thing that means the most to me." He described it to Ann this way--"It's a piece of the parachute that I jumped into France with. I cut a big chunk out of my chute as I landed & [in] every town that we took, the women wanted a piece of parachute. That is the size of the piece I wound up with. I had a scarf made of it in Nice & had the initials embroidered on it." The initials, of course, were Ann's, "AF," with "France 1944" embroidered above them. (Dick still has the scarf today. The red embroidered letters appear as bright in color as they must have been in 1944.) Dick's interest in photography also is apparent in an analysis of the items he sent home. In a "small box" and in a "shell case," he mailed for safekeeping pictures and negatives from his time in Sicily, Italy, and southern France. One of the photographs was a large print of the historic daytime combat jump on August 15, 1944.

Dick included, too, a camera that took "slides instead of rolls." Aside from the scarf made from his parachute, a second gift for Ann was a "heavy bracelet" from Oran that Dick stored in his duffel bag for over a year. He put the other souvenirs he collected in the same bag. The Army stored it for Dick when he was on the move, such as in southern France, the Maritime Alps, and the Ardennes. As Dick put it, the duffel bag "followed me around." Somehow, it caught up with him when his unit was stationed in a more permanent location, such as Laon. The Army sent Dick and his duffel bag next to the French town of Epinal, near Nancy.[284]

At the end of July 1945, the 82nd left France for its new assignment as part of the occupation forces in Berlin. The 40 and 8s again proved to be the mode of transportation. The train ride took five days, with various units arriving in the German capital between August 1st and the 8th.[285] In a letter to Ann on August 17, 1945, Dick told her he was now in Berlin after what he characterized as "a miserable ride." The boxcars still did not carry water containers from which the men could refill their canteens. Additionally, the 40 and 8s remained without any toilet facilities. If there was a bright note for Dick after his unit arrived in Germany's capital, it would have been the news of Japan's surrender on August 10th. He recalls that "everyone felt a great sense of relief." The 82nd would not be sent to the Pacific Theater. Home seemed much closer after V-J Day (Victory Over Japan).

Like the country of Germany itself, Berlin had been divided among the Allies into four zones of occupation--the American, the British, the French, and the Soviet Zones. Located within the last area, Berlin became a magnet for deserters from the Soviet Army. The men roamed the streets in armed gangs. Soviet troops who remained in the military posed threats as well because of their unruly behavior. The 82nd was ordered to guard the outer perimeter of the American Zone within the city.[286] Dick characterizes their military presence as one "for show." As he puts it, the troopers "stood on street corners" where they wore "white parachute shroud lines for bootlaces" and "white gloves." Their guns had no ammunition in them. Soon, though, a complaint by Dick to a superior officer resulted in his reassignment.

Division replacements arrived from the United States. Dick explained the gulf between them and the veteran members of the 82nd in a short sentence, "We had been in combat and they had not." One sergeant who came in from the States irritated Dick to such a degree that he approached his company commander (CO). Pointing out the experience he had from his time in the ETO, Dick explained the frustration he felt having to take orders from the new sergeant who did not have his background. Dick believed the sergeant resented the time others had spent in combat. The man's abrasive personality only aggravated how he dealt with the enlisted men under him. Dick's request of the CO was a simple one. He wanted a new duty assignment where he would not have to deal with the sergeant. The officer sympathized with Dick and gave him what he wanted. His new orders were to set up what some might call a recreation hall for the enlisted men. Dick calls it "a beer hall." It would be his duty station for the rest of his time in Berlin. There would be entertainment at the hall as well as beer, both of which Dick was in charge of procuring. His CO allowed him to choose some enlisted soldiers from his company to work under him. As an added bonus, he did not have to bunk anymore with the rest of his platoon. Instead, Dick slept on a cot in a room at the end of the hall.

He set up the recreation hall in a district on the western side of Berlin, known as the Wannsee section of the city. Dick classifies it as a "well-to-do area." The Havel River flowed by two adjacent lakes and a man-made beach. Berliners knew the Wannsee as a recreational spot because of the outdoor opportunities it offered. With his background in Liberty, New York, Dick must have felt very much at home in such a location. Abandoned mansions stood in the community, and Dick found a Steinway baby grand piano in one of them. He and his men loaded it onto a truck, delivering it to the Army's recreation hall. Dick played it for the soldiers. As other forms of entertainment, he set up a volleyball court and an area in which soldiers could pitch horseshoes. The beer probably proved a greater attraction than the piano or games. Dick and his assistants used an Army truck to pick up the beer, stored in wooden kegs with spigots,

119

from a local brewery. While writing a letter to Ann one day, Dick took a short break. He shared with his wife the reason behind it-- "Pardon me, Honey. They just tapped a beer keg out back so I'm going to get some." Once he picked up the pen again, he added "Well, this stuff is nothing like Weiss's [a New York City tavern], but it will do."[287] Looking back at this assignment, Dick explains that those months resulted in some "wild times." While he much preferred this

duty to standing guard in other parts of the city, what he really wanted was to go home. He never stopped telling Ann that in his letters. It had been a theme in them even before V-E Day, and now with demobilization, Dick referred to it even more. Once the 82nd arrived in Berlin, the Army delivered mail to the division. It had been almost a month since Dick received a letter from his wife. In his first letter to her from the German capital, Dick vented his frustration. They had been apart for about sixteen months. He wrote Ann, "If I'm away from you much longer, I'll go bugs. I'm just burning inside to get away from all this. It's worse than prison. True, we got a pretty good deal here [the recreation hall assignment], but the one I love most is not here, so what's the good of it?"[288]

In his first month in Berlin, Dick received a seven-day furlough. He had a choice of one of three cities--Brussels, Paris, or Nice. He chose the last one because he had helped to liberate it. He explained his reasoning to Ann, "I'll get to look over the old places without having to worry about getting shot at."[289] Joe Killgore, his old squad leader in the 551st who also had been re-assigned to the 505th, accompanied him. They hitched a ride in a C-47 whose flight to Nice lasted five and a half hours. The troopers stayed at the Negresco Hotel, where a Frenchman who Dick identifies as "a sidewalk photographer" snapped a picture of the two men. During their stay, Dick watched with amusement some women he passed in the streets.

It was their clothing that caught his eye. They had "a blouse or a skirt made from a parachute." After he returned to Berlin, two packages from his mother awaited him. Dick summarized in a September 1st letter to Esther how much he had enjoyed his return to Nice--"I really had a swell time. The place is sure changed since I was down there last time. You sleep in luxurious hotels with plenty of service, good beer, ice cream, cognac, nightclubs, and you can really have a good time." In the letter, he enclosed the picture of himself and Joe in front of the hotel.

The "good time" Dick enjoyed while on furlough probably increased his desire to be out of the Army even more. Just as he had written to Ann about how anxious he was to go home, that theme appeared, too, in the September 1st letter to his mother. Dick openly told her that he was "pretty disgusted with this whole dammed affair over here. Now that the other mess is over [the Pacific war], I'm kind of anxious to get home…" Apparently his brother Archie was already in the States or on his way there. Dick complained to his mother, "Boy, I wish I was in Archie's shoes. He sure hit it lucky, didn't he? I wish to hell I could get just one break out of this Army." Dick's "break" finally came in October. Exactly one month after he had written the above letter to Esther, he penned another one. This one had a much more positive tone to it. On October 1st he announced to his mother, "I have some good news. This Christmas might be a little better than the last two I've had. I expect to be home by Xmas. Boy, you don't know how happy that makes me. What a hole this place is. I'll sure be glad to get out of here." Dick was now to be officially part of what the military called "demobilization."

Even before the Germans officially surrendered in May, General Marshall approved a plan that created a formula to determine the order in which servicemen would be discharged. (The War Department rejected an earlier idea to discharge by unit. It chose to release the men on an individual basis.) The demobilization plan was based upon a point system. Each member of the military received points for time in the service, time spent overseas, time in combat, the number of wounds received, and the number of children the serviceman had waiting for him Stateside. The point system began operation in May 1945 when the war in Europe ended. Between V-E Day and V-J Day, almost 600,000 men had been discharged. In the fall of 1945, the War Department exceeded its own estimations on how many members of the military it would be able to "boot out." In September the number reached 597,000. October saw 1,270,000 discharged. The monthly total declined somewhat in November, to 1,186,000. Dick became one of the December numbers--1,112,000. General Eisenhower admitted that Washington was making "every effort to get as many men home for Christmas with their families as was humanly possible." By mid-January 1946, five million had passed through what the military called "separation centers." In a speech before a Joint Session of Congress on January 15, 1946, Eisenhower concluded, "Certainly there has never been such a planned movement of men over great distances in the history of any nation." The demobilization rate, however, declined in the new year. As Eisenhower explained, if the rate seen in the last months of 1945 continued, the military would "run out of an army."[290]

On November 19, 1945, the military relieved the 82nd Airborne Division of its occupation duty in Berlin. The troopers were returning to the States, some, like Dick, to be discharged. After being trucked to a train station, they departed the German capital in the same way they had traveled throughout much of Europe, in 40 and 8s. The railroad cars took the men first back to Camp Chicago outside of Laon. From there they went to Camp Lucky Strike near the French port of La Havre, France.[291] After the German occupation of Normandy ended in the summer of 1944, the Allies set up camps around La Havre where an airfield, used by the French and Germans, stood. The site processed soldiers for their return to the United States, temporarily housed men on leave, and served as a staging area to transfer troops from the European to the Pacific Theater if that ever proved necessary. The military named the transit camps after American cigarettes, such as Camp Camel, Camp Pall Mall, and Camp Chesterfield. The 82nd ended up at the largest of these, Camp Lucky Strike. Situated on approximately two and a half acres, the Army Corps of Engineers erected more than twelve thousand large, olive drab tents on both sides of what had been a runway. The airstrip became the main boulevard in the camp. The tents, with wooden floors, offered American soldiers beds with pillows and fresh sheets; showers stood nearby. Camp Lucky Strike alone had been equipped to handle about fifty-eight thousand men, but each week one hundred thousand might be found there. Once he arrived at Camp Lucky Strike, Dick emphasizes that he was no longer part of the 82nd Airborne Division. In his words, in order "to keep a paper trail" on each man, the Army assigned soldiers to any one of several units. Dick is not sure if he was given over to an artillery, engineering, or quartermaster unit. If not one of those, Dick ended up, at least on paper, in some unit. Such a transfer allowed the military to list him somewhere in a camp that housed tens of thousands of men in transit to someplace. Like his fellow soldiers, Dick availed himself of the camp's amenities--movie theaters, mess halls that served ice cream and hot dogs, Red Cross stations, and even bars that opened for three hours in the evenings.[292] Dick frequented all of these except for the last one.

While some members of the 82nd left Camp Lucky Strike for England where they boarded ships to take them home, the Army sent Dick back to the States by a different route. Sometime at the end of November, Dick climbed onto a train that headed south to the Rhone River Valley. Unlike his other European railroad trips, on this one Dick sat in a coach car. He disembarked at Marseilles. Dick found the harbor to be "a mess." Several damaged ships sat in the port, perhaps hit a year earlier by enemy bombs or scuttled by the Allies now that the war was over. Along with other soldiers destined for the States, Dick boarded a ship. At one point before he did so, though, Dick got out a telegram to Ann. Dated December 1, 1945, the short message told her, "Chance to be home Xmas but don't count on it."

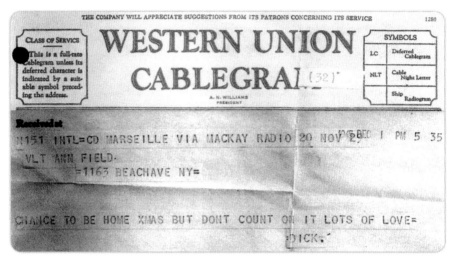

As he had in May 1944, Dick watched from the deck as the vessel passed through the Straits of Gibraltar. As he points out, he entered Europe through southern France and now left it through the same area. Because of the time of year, December instead of April/May, this trip proved much rougher than his voyage over to the ETO. Dick classifies it as "a real, real bad crossing." The weather was "terrible," with seas so rough that the soldiers had to eat their meals on the deck rather than in the mess hall below, perhaps to facilitate the cleanup from spilled food. The trip home did have two redeeming aspects. First, the voyage from Europe to the United States did not take as long as Dick's first transatlantic crossing; there was no need to observe a zip zag approach when the ship neared land. Second, the vessel Dick sailed on was not part of a convoy that included very slow ships. It traveled by itself, and thus maintained a higher speed than if it were sailing with other vessels.

His ship docked in Boston Harbor. From there, the Army transported Dick to Camp Miles Standish in Taunton, Massachusetts. With December 25th approaching, Dick was given a choice--he could go home right away to insure that he would be with his family for Christmas, and then return to the camp to be formally discharged, or, he could stay in camp to await the processing of his separation papers. Because Dick wanted out of the Army "as soon as possible," he passed on the immediate trip home. With his discharge papers signed on December 26, 1945, Dick left for New York City by train, dressed as a soldier but officially a civilian. After a subway ride, he went first to his dad's shop. Father and son ended up at Weiss's Tavern, after which Archie took Dick to the von Hagen family's apartment on Beach Avenue. Ann had lived with her parents during Dick's service in Europe. When she knew, however, that he would be returning to the States, she rented a small apartment just for them. But on the day of his arrival in New York City, Dick had no idea as to its location. It turned out to be just three or four blocks from Beach Avenue. On that 26th day of December in 1945, Ann was at her parent's home when her husband arrived. After a twenty-month separation, Dick and Ann were finally together again.

Chapter 12

Epilogue

Dick Field's World War II experience is perhaps best summarized with two words, "sacrifice" and "service." These words are applicable, of course, to millions of his peers who were also in the United States military. But with Dick, we can see the toll that his service took on him through the letters he sent home. Others in uniform wrote loved ones, too. Esther and Ann, however, did what many recipients did not do. They saved the correspondence. Dick's written observations, and the feelings he shared with his mother and wife, allow his story to be documented to a degree that is not possible for most members of his generation. His letters speak to his service as a member of a parachute infantry battalion--the specialized trooper training that taught him how to jump out of an airplane and land properly, his continued months of infantry training after he arrived in Europe, his participation in Operation Dragoon, the months spent in the Maritime Alps, his weeks of intense combat in the Ardennes, the movement across the Rhine as well as the Elbe River, and finally, his last months in the ETO, spent in Berlin.

The letters also address the frustration of being separated from his wife. Dick and Ann had been married only a few weeks when he shipped out. It is understandable that his favorite World War II song is one whose theme focuses on the wartime separation of couples, "We'll Meet Again." His correspondence home, though, speaks to other separations, specifically the attachments and detachments of his independent battalion to larger units. Such actions denied Dick and all members of the 551st a strong sense of belonging to regiments and divisions they became a part of. That feeling was probably mutual when it came to how other units related to the "bastard battalion." Dick had become part of a tight-knit "family," as he describes the 551st, when he joined the unit in December 1943. That family began to vanish before his eyes as its casualties mounted during the Battle of the Bulge. In January 1946 on the fields below Rochelinval, it almost completely disappeared as its ranks became even smaller. Gavin's announcement to the survivors later that month of the unit's deactivation only validated what Dick had witnessed during his time in the Ardennes. Men who had served together for a year as members of the 551st suddenly found themselves assigned to other units. Separated from his wife for months, and then his military family forever, Dick did not start the New Year of 1945 on a high note. His service ended, though, in December of that year with his discharge from the Army. He celebrated New Year's Day in 1946 as a civilian and no longer apart from the woman he loved.

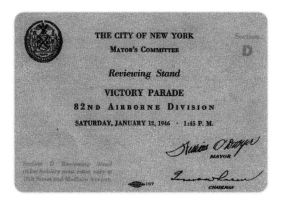

About a week after Dick's return, he received a special invitation in the mail. The New York City mayor's office requested his attendance at a Victory Parade down Fifth Avenue, scheduled for Saturday, January 12, 1946. The 82nd Airborne Division would be formally welcomed home. The envelope contained two tickets. Strangely, though, the organizers of the event were not inviting Dick to march in the parade. Instead, the tickets were for seating in "Section D" of the "Reviewing Stand." At the time, Dick did not think anything of this. On the 12th, he showed up in his paratrooper's uniform, including his distinctive boots. The left sleeve of his jacket displayed the 82nd Airborne Division patch. General Gavin led almost nine thousand troopers in the parade. Even though the temperature was just in the forties, with a possibility of rain, an estimated two to four million people stood on the streets to welcome the paratroopers home. In the sky above the city, forty C-47s flew, each one towing a glider.[293] Because Dick arrived late, he would have had to cross Fifth Avenue, in front of the marching veterans, to reach the reviewing stands. A member of the *Daily News*, a city newspaper, saw Dick in his uniform. He was on a scaffold where reporters and crews with

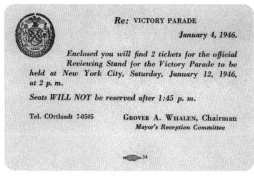

Re: VICTORY PARADE

January 4, 1946.

Enclosed you will find 2 tickets for the official Reviewing Stand for the Victory Parade to be held at New York City, Saturday, January 12, 1946, at 2 p. m.

Seats WILL NOT be reserved after 1:45 p. m.

Tel. COrtlandt 7-0505   GROVER A. WHALEN, Chairman
Mayor's Reception Committee

movie cameras were perched to document the parade in word and film. One of them invited Dick to join them for an elevated view of the event. He took the man up on the offer. After the march ended, Dick attended a reception for members of the 82nd at a hotel. Then he went home to Ann.

For a few years, the young couple lived in New York City. Dick worked with his father at Archie's automobile repair shop. Like millions of other veterans, Dick moved on after the war. They had done what they invariably call their "job." Now, in the postwar years, it was time to put the war behind them. It had been a defining moment in their lives. At the time, however, many if not most did not understand that fact. Dick admits today that back then, right after the war, "I never thought it was a big deal." Beginning in 1946, Dick had other parts of his life to live. The war was behind his generation and the future in front of them. Demographers point to "the Baby Boom" that started in 1946 as couples began having families after the war ended. The Fields contributed to that climb in the birth rate. In the fall of 1946, he and Ann welcomed their first child, a son, named Richard J. Field, Jr. But "Rick," as the baby came to be called, developed asthma. A doctor recommended a change of climate for the family. In 1948 or 1949, Dick took his family back home to Liberty. He worked at a Nash dealership for a few years as "a working service manager." Dick managed the shop and repaired cars. The Field family grew by one more in 1950 with the birth of their daughter Virginia ("Ginni"). It did not take long, however, for the upward and downward swings of the local economy to become all too apparent to Dick. With tourism its only business, residents of Liberty did well in the summer months as people came in and out of the town. But in the winter, financially they just "got by," as Dick puts it. He saw "no future in the town" for himself. The Fields relocated to a place that became famous in the history of post World War II America--Levittown, Pennsylvania.

Just like the birth of Dick and Ann's children made them part of the postwar Baby Boom, the Fields' move to Levittown made them part of the postwar migration to the suburbs with their planned communities. Real estate businessman William J. Levitt built housing developments that carried his name, Levittown. Dick and Ann moved to the one in Pennsylvania when Dick got a job as a line mechanic at the Johnson Oldsmobile dealership in Trenton, New Jersey. During World War II, the Levitt and Sons construction company received a government contract to build over two thousand housing units for defense workers in Norfolk, Virginia. After the war ended, the Levitts applied techniques they used in wartime mass housing construction to building homes in postwar America. They opened their first development on Long Island in 1947. Dick's brother Archie bought a

home there. Levittown, Pennsylvania followed five years later. It became one of the largest planned communities in the country. Levitt and

Sons built over seventeen thousand houses in its Bucks Country development. Dick and Ann owned one of them. He remembers their home cost less than nine thousand dollars, with a monthly payment of around fifty dollars. That was the typical cost and mortgage payment for houses in Levittown, Pennsylvania.[294] Since that community was located just across the river from Trenton, Dick could easily commute to work. During his time at Johnson Olds, he worked "side-by-side," as he puts it, with Howard Adcock. The two talked as they fixed cars, but never about the war years. Ironically, even though Dick did not know it at the time, Howard had served in the 551st Parachute Infantry Battalion, too, but in a different company than his. Dick did not realize this until decades later when he was looking at photographs of members of the 551st in a book that came out in 1984.

While living in Levittown, Dick began to receive more than one job promotion. After about two years as a line mechanic, he became an assistant service manager for Johnson Olds. Dick left that job, though, for one as a full service manager at a Chrysler-Plymouth dealership in Morrisville, Pennsylvania, near Levittown. During these years in Bucks County, Ann worked in the Levitt and Sons' mortgage department. A neighbor watched Rick and Ginni. In 1958, Dick became a car salesman for the dealership. That same year, Levitt and Sons began selling homes in one of its new communities, Levittown, New Jersey, not far from the development in Pennsylvania. Because of Ann's position with the company, she and Dick were able to select a house in this third Levittown when it was still in the development stages. After looking over blueprints of the new community, the Fields chose a larger home than the one they owned in Pennsylvania. The New Jersey residence also stood on a lot that measured about half an acre. They remained in the new Levittown for almost twenty years while Dick worked at the Chrysler-Plymouth dealership and Ann in the mortgage department for Levitt and Sons. Once the New Jersey development sold out the home sites, the construction company closed its offices there. Ann did not look for another position. She stayed home with Rick and Ginni.

Dick never went into detail with either of his children about his wartime service. It did, however, factor into one piece of advice Dick gave his son. After high school, Rick "dawdled," as his father puts it. American involvement in the Vietnam War was escalating. With the draft in effect, Dick knew his son had to either enroll in college or take the chance of being put into the military. Since continuing his formal education did not appeal to Rick, his father urged him to enlist in the Air Force or the Navy. After life as an infantryman in the ETO, Dick stressed the benefits of "three squares a day" and "a bunk with clean sheets." As he lectured his son, "I'm speaking from experience." Rick chose the Navy. It trained him in electronics. That area of expertise seemed a natural one for Rick, given his paternal grandfather and father's mechanical abilities. As it turned out, he spent twenty years in the Navy. For almost all of that time, Rick served as a crewman on a P-3A Orion, a surveillance aircraft. In the early 1970s, he ended up at Naval Air Station North Island, in San Diego.

In 1976, Dick and Ann moved to Oceanside, California. By that time, Dick was in his fifties. The half acre lot that had appealed to him and Ann in Levittown, New Jersey now seemed like a burden. The yard needed constant attention. Additionally, his feet still felt the effects of the 1944-1945 Belgian winter. The cold weather on the East Coast aggravated circulation problems. With Rick based at North Island, Dick and Ann decided to relocate to that area. Don Sharp Volkswagen in Carlsbad, a coastal community north of San Diego, hired him as a salesman. Dick quickly became a sales manager. When Bob Baker bought the dealership in 1982, Dick stayed on in that position. Later Baker added Chrysler and Plymouth cars to the showrooms. It turned out that Bob Baker had served as part of the airborne forces in the Korean War. He regularly received the *Static Line* magazine, a publication directed toward those who had been in airborne operations or were interested in them. After reading it, Baker passed on copies to his new employee.

In one of the issues, Dick saw a column on the 551st and an upcoming reunion. He had no idea that his battalion had begun holding such gatherings. The first one occurred in 1977, with twenty-four paratroopers and family members in attendance.[295] The first reunion Dick attended was in June 1982 in King of Prussia, Pennsylvania, near Valley Forge. Ann accompanied him. Eight years later, Dick went to Washington, D.C. to participate in the fiftieth anniversary of the American airborne forces. The celebration was part of the fourteenth annual reunion of airborne groups, held on July 4th-

9th. Various units paraded down Pennsylvania Avenue. Dick had the privilege of carrying the United States flag as the men marched. His friend Joe Cicchinelli carried the 551st battalion flag. Ann watched from within the crowd.

A reunion of the 551st in the year 2000 carries particular significance for Dick. By that date, some troopers had passed away, but family members often still showed up at the gatherings. The son of a veteran did so that year. He was an attorney and had a contact who worked at the Veterans Administration. The lawyer offered to help Dick locate some of his buddies from the war. Dick only asked for information on one of them, Marshall Clay. A few weeks later, Dick received what appeared to be Marshall's current address, a post office box in Arizona. (He later found out that Marshall lived on an Indian reservation, in Keams Canyon.) Dick wrote him a letter, enclosing photographs of himself and the Marshall Clay he had served with in the ETO. Dick asked if the Clay to whom he was now writing was the Clay from Company B in the 551st. Marshall's daughter wrote back. Yes, the soldier in the pictures was her father. She told Dick that his letter touched her dad. Marshall felt that no one in the unit would remember him. Dick urged the Clay family to attend the next reunion, to be held in San Diego in October 2001. They did. Although his wife had died, Marshall came with his son and two daughters, along with some of their spouses. The Clay family knew it was going to meet the man who had saved their father's life on the bluff at Rochelinval.

The meeting for Dick and Marshall was an emotional one. It had been almost fifty-seven years since the two paratroopers had last seen each other. Marshall shared with his friend memories of January 7, 1945 and what happened to him after he arrived at the aid station in Dairomont. In respect to his injury, Marshall recalled only "a big explosion." The next thing he remembered was waking up with his "head full of bandages." Marshall told Dick that he spent about eight months in Army hospitals. He underwent more than one plastic surgery to repair the damage the German mortar round had caused. After his discharge, Marshall returned home where he became a tribal policeman on the reservation. Even though the 551st Parachute Infantry Association installed Dick as its president at that San Diego gathering, the real highlight for Dick was his reunion with Marshall. As it turned out, it would be the last time the two men saw each other. The Navajo Indian veteran died in February of 2005. While Dick belongs to a national association of Veterans of the Battle of the Bulge, he has never attended one of their reunions. It is the 551st that he wants to honor by keeping the memory of its World War II service alive.

Other veterans of the battalion feel the same way. One in particular, Dan Morgan, spent four years documenting the history of the 551st. He began this monumental task in 1980, but immediately became frustrated. Official government and military archives he visited had few records of the 551st. So in 1982 Morgan went from state to state to interview over ninety men who had served in the unit. He traveled fourteen thousand miles in four months, spending two or three days with each man. Aside from these recollections, he drew upon photographs, unclassified battalion records some of the veterans had, letters the men had written home during the war, diary entries, and even some unpublished memoirs. Morgan pulled all of this together in a book, one which he stressed "is truly theirs [the men of the 551st], for it is they who finally brought our ghost back to life." He self-published the volume in 1984. Entitled *The Left Corner of My Heart, The Saga of the 551st Parachute Infantry Battalion*, it takes its name from the dedication Morgan wrote to Colonel Wood Joerg. In it, he concluded that to the troopers, the colonel was "father, uncle, older brother, comrade. He shared everything with us--the good along with the bad." Morgan continued by describing the mutual feelings the men had for their leader, and his feelings for them, as ones of "love." But it was only after Joerg's death at Rochelinval, in Morgan's words, "did each of us find deep in the innermost corner of our hearts just how much we loved him."[296]

The special affection battalion members feel for Joerg can also be seen in a monument to the 551st that stands today in Rochelinval. Dignitaries gathered in August of 1989 to dedicate a bronze plaque

embedded in a large rock. Two Belgian men were the prime forces behind the monument. One had been a resistance leader during the war, and the other a young man raised in Rochelinval who became fascinated with the story of the 551st. Colonel Joerg's photograph is fixed into the stone above the plaque. An American and Belgian flag fly over the monument.

With the passage of time, the 551st has been remembered with other memorials--a marble tablet installed in 1988 at the doorway of St. Martin Vesubie's City Hall in southern France, a stone marker dedicated in 1990 at the start of the walkway that leads to the Tomb of the Unknown Soldier in Arlington National Cemetery, a monument dedicated in 2000 at Draguignan in France, a stone at Fort Benning's Airborne Walk, and bronze memorials in the Belgian towns of

Noirefontaine and Leignon.[297] A small plaque is even mounted on the wall of the chapel that still stands on the grounds of the Stevens Estate, the 551st's landing site on Operation Dragoon's D-Day. There is also, as noted earlier, a memorial to the troopers killed in the

training accident at Camp MacKall and a street in Draguignan named for the battalion. The foregoing is not meant to be a complete list, but it is representative of recent attempts to remember the unit. The independent battalion played significant roles in Operation Dragoon, the Battle of the Bulge, and the crossing of the Elbe. The unit history of the 551st Parachute Infantry Battalion should be acknowledged.

But until recently, the 551st was even overlooked when it came to military honors. Major Bill Holm, who commanded the battalion after Joerg's death, recommended it for the Distinguished Unit Citation early in 1945. The High Command took no action on his request. Admirers resurrected the recommendation decades later. It was formally conferred upon the 551st at a Pentagon ceremony in February 2001. The Presidential Unit Citation with Valor referred to "heroic actions" that took place January 3-7, 1945. Those were the days, of course, when the 551st acted as the "tip of the spearhead" of the Allied counteroffensive in the Bulge. Dick attended the 2001 Pentagon ceremony. Ann, their son, and daughter-in-law looked on. In respect to military honors, another glaring omission occurred with the Belgian Croix de Guerre. The 82nd failed to list the 551st when reporting to the Belgian government units that had fought in the Battle of the Bulge. It appears that only the French government recognized when it should have the contributions of the 551st. It conferred the French Croix de Guerre on the paratroopers in July 1946.[298]

That is one of the military recognitions conferred upon Dick for his wartime service. It is hung, with others, in assorted frames and cases on a wall in his home today. Most prominently displayed are the Expert Rifleman Badge, the Combat Infantry Badge, the Good Conduct Medal, the European-African-Middle Eastern Campaign Medal with four stars and an arrowhead (which represents four campaigns and a combat parachute jump, respectively), the Bronze Star, the Belgian Fourragere, the French Legion of Honor (France's highest award), the Presidential Unit Citation with an oak leaf cluster that signifies Dick's membership in two units that were so recognized (the 551st and the 505th), the World War II Army of Occupation (Germany), and the World War II Victory Medal. Dick never received a Purple Heart. In jest, he concludes, "I guess I knew how to duck real well." On a more serious note, Dick points out that in spite of the fact he spent two months in hospitals due to severe frostbite, that type of casualty condition did not qualify for a Purple Heart. Dick had to "bleed," as he puts it, to receive one of those medals. In addition to all of these awards, several medallions lay on some shelves in the same room of Dick's home where the other military awards hang. French and Belgian villages liberated by the 551st presented them to veterans of the unit decades after the war was over.

In recent years, Dick educates younger generations on the role of the 551st in World War II. In San Diego's North County, he visits local high schools and college classes to share his personal history. In the summers, Dick regularly attends the graduation ceremony at a private jump school in Frederick, Oklahoma. He answers questions

about what it was like to train and serve as a paratrooper in the war. Dick also takes part, when he can, in a Washington, D.C. event that commemorates Operation Dragoon. Organized by a retired Army officer, it is held in August at Arlington National Cemetery. In some years, however, Dick missed that gathering so he could be in southern France to observe Dragoon's anniversary where it actually happened. Over the last few decades, Dick has returned to France and Belgium more than once. One memorable trip occurred in November 1996 when he and Joe Killgore visited cities and villages they had helped to liberate in the summer and fall of 1944. His daughter Ginni accompanied him on his last few trips. (Rick passed away in 2003 and Ann in 2008.) When asked why he returns so often, Dick replied, "It was a tremendous time in my life. When I go back, I relive it. And the French and Belgian people have a lot to do with it. They are so grateful." Ironically, the 551st seems to be recognized for its service more in the French and Belgian towns and villages it helped to liberate than in books that chronicle the history of World War II.

Those who have studied the story of the 551st in detail believe that the very strength of the unit--its independency--contributed to the military's slighting of its wartime contributions. The battalion displayed a maverick spirit, from its leaders down to the enlisted men. Early in his research, Dan Morgan became frustrated at his inability to find documentation of the 551st in various archival collections. He emphasized that, "the pertinent Battalion records appear to have been destroyed or lost in some manner." In 1980 when Morgan poured over records of specific airborne units, such as the 82nd and the 505th, he found "only an occasional reference to the 551st" when it should have figured prominently in the documents. Morgan continued, "There is no mention anywhere of the Battalion's attack on Rochelinval, nor of the near-annihilation of the Battalion." Such omissions led Morgan to a powerful conclusion--"Looking back from this very distant time, I feel compelled to say that it seems likely to me that there were persons in the staff sections of regimental, division-level or both, who systematically struck down or degraded the activities of the 551st Battalion." Analysis was Morgan's forte. After the war, he worked for over twenty years with the Central Intelligence Agency as an analyst. Whether such omissions resulted from what he called "incompetence," "callousness," or "deliberate malice," he did not know. Morgan hoped that his book would correct those slights, and "secure for the 551st the recognition it earned."[299]

Within such a context, the failure of organizers behind New York City's Victory Parade to invite Dick to march with the 82nd Airborne Division appears not at all surprising. During the parade, and at a reception for members of the division afterwards, Dick noticed that many of those who marched were replacements. Most of those in the parade, according to Dick, had not been with the All American Division throughout its time in the ETO. Some who marched had not even been with it for the length of time Dick had. The High Command attached the 551st Parachute Infantry Battalion to the 82nd during the Battle of the Bulge. After Dick's discharge from the hospital in England, the Army assigned him to the 82nd on a permanent basis. He served with the division for almost a year, until his discharge a month before the parade. Yet for some strange reason, Dick was not invited to march with the 82nd Airborne Division in the Victory Parade. His service warranted only a seat in the reviewing stands, not full participation in the event. On that cold, overcast January day in 1946, Dick stood on the periphery as New York City honored his division. In a way, that is how the service of the 551st stands in history--on the edge, not front and center. Until recently, the independent battalion was largely forgotten, except, of course, by men such as Dick Field who served in it.

Endnotes

[1] Population figures for Liberty and New York City are taken from the Works Projects Administration (WPA) Guides for New York State, *New York: A Guide to the Empire State* (New York, 1940), p. 386 and *The WPA Guide to New York City* (New York, 1939), p. 3 respectively. Information on Dick's parents and his early years are from conversations with the author in July and August 2010. Details on Dick's training and service in the ETO are taken from discussions in September 2010. Dick shared his experiences in the ETO with the author in June 2011-January 2012. Unless otherwise noted, all quotations from Dick are taken from conversation between him and the author.

[2] http://www.sullivancountyhistory.org

[3] Archie entered his birth year as 1890 on his World War I registration card, and "about 1890" is entered on a similar line for "Esther Field" in the 1930 census. Both documents available on http:www.ancestry.com.

[4] Copy of booklet, belonging to Dick Field, in possession of author.

[5] Jonathan Zimmerman, *Small Wonder: The Little Red Schoolhouse in History and Memory* (New Haven, 2009), p. 30.

[6] Writers' Program of the Works Projects Administration, *New York: A Guide to the Empire State* (New York, 1940), p. 132.

[7] The 1930 census lists thirteen-year-old Mary Dexheimer as part of the Arch Field household. http:www.ancestry.com.

[8] Writers' Program of the Works Projects Administration, *New York* [State], p. 386. The WPA Guide notes the "sanatorium" and the resort facilities as Liberty's main attractions.

[9] The topography of Liberty is described in James Eldridge Quinlan, *History of Sullivan County* (Liberty, 1873), pp. 327-328.

[10] Writers' Program of the Works Projects Administration, *New York* [State], p. 386.

[11] Federal Writer's Project, *The WPA Guide to New York City* (New York, 1939), p. 3.

[12] Writers' Program of the Works Projects Administration, *New York* [State], p. 267.

[13] Ibid.

[14] Writers' Program of the Works Projects Administration, *New York* [State], p. 134.

[15] Ibid.

[16] Federal Writer's Project, *The WPA Guide to New York City*, p.401.

[17] Ibid., p. 548.

[18] Ibid., p. 549.

[19] Writers' Program of the Works Projects Administration, *New York* [State], p. xxii.

[20] Ibid., p.202.

[21] John C. McManus, *The Deadly Brotherhood: The American Combat Soldier in World War II* (New York, 1998), p. 9.

Two publications from 1944 explain the induction process in detail. One is entitled *Answers to Important Questions for the Potential Inductee and His*

Dependents, published by the Oregon State Defense Council. Information in it was compiled by the Army Service Forces. A second one is *Introduction to the Armed Forces: Suggestions for Pre-Induction Informational Meetings,* published by the U.S. Office of Civil Defense. Both are available at http://arcweb.sos.state.or.us/exhibits/ww2/services/induct.htm (accessed June 17, 2011).

The details on Dick's experiences at the Induction Station and the Reception Center are taken from his recollections and from the above two 1944 publications.

[22] Dick Field to Ann von Hagen, June 15, 1943. Copy in possession of author.

[23] Dick Field to Ann von Hagen, June 17, 1943 refers to his thirteen weeks of training. On the envelope of his June 15th letter, Dick identifies his placement in the 1st Platoon, Co. A, 12th Training Battalion. Copies.

[24] http://formercampwheeler.com/history.htm (accessed October 11, 2010). Camp Wheeler closed in 1946, at which time the government returned the land to its original owners.

[25] Dick Field to Ann von Hagen, June 15, 1943. Copy.

[26] Dick Field to Ann von Hagen, June 17, 1943. Copy.

[27] Ibid.

[28] Ibid.

[29] Ibid.

[30] Gordon L. Rottman, *US Combat Engineer 1941-45* (New York, 2010), p. 19 gives 0500 hours, or 5:00 A.M., as reveille.

[31] Dick Field to Ann von Hagen, undated letter from Camp Wheeler. Copy.

[32] Dick Field to Mrs. A.L. Field, July 8, 1943. Copy.

[33] The outlines of BT is taken from Col. Raymond H. Bluhm, Jr., USA (Ret.) and Col. James B. Motley, USA (Ret.), *The Soldier's Guidebook* (Washington, 1995), pp. 44-54.

[34] Dick Field to Ann Von Hagen, June 24, 1943. Copy.

[35] Ibid.

[36] Dick Field to Mrs. A.L. Field, July 8, 1943. Copy.

[37] Rottman, *US Combat Engineer*, p. 19 identifies taps at 2200 hours.

[38] Dick Field to Mrs. A.L. Field, July 8, 1943. Copy.

[39] The uniform of a paratrooper is described well in Ed Ruggero, *Combat Jump: The Young Men Who Led the Assault into Fortress Europe, July 1943* (New York, 2003), pp. 23-24.

[40] Dick Field to Mrs. A.L. Field, October 29, 1943. Copy. Dick complained about not receiving any letters "in a couple of weeks because of being shipped around so much."

[41] The airport is identified as Lawson Field in Gregory Orfalea, *Messengers of the Lost Battalion: The Heroic 551st and the Turning of the Tide at the Battle of the Bulge* (New York, 1997), p. 39.

[42] Phil Nordyke, *All American, All the Way: The Combat History of the 82nd Airborne Division in World War II* (St. Paul, MN, 2005), p. 17. Dick judges this book to be "on the mark" when it comes to the story of the 82nd.

[43] Ibid.

[44] Ibid., p. 7 for these "graduation requirements" and for the eight-nine hour day.

[45] Ibid., p. 10.

[46] Dick Field to Mrs. A.L. Field, November 18, 1943. Copy.

[47] Dick Field to Mrs. A.L. Field, November 18, 1943. Copy.

[48] Ibid.

[49] Nordyke, *All American,* pp. 8-9.

[50] Dick Field to Mrs. A.L. Field, November 18, 1943. Copy.

[51] Ibid., p.8.

[52] Dick Field to Mrs. A.L. Field, November 27, 1943. Copy.

[53] Orfalea, *Messengers of the Lost Battalion*, p. 70.

[54] Ibid., pp. 45-67 details the mission of the 551st in Panama.

[55] Ibid., pp. xvi, 204. The other battalion was the 509th.

[56] A battalion had between 600-800 men and a company about 150. Ibid., p. 16.

[57] Dick Field to Mrs. A.L. Field, December 12, 1943. Copy.

[58] Ibid.

[59] Orfalea, *Messengers of the Lost Battalion*, pp. 75-77.

[60] Dick Field to Mrs. A.L. Field, December 12, 1943. Copy.

[61] Dick Field to Mrs. A.L. Field, December 26, 1943. Copy.

[62] Orfalea, *Messengers of the Lost Battalion*, p. 76.

[63] Ibid.

[64] Ibid., p. 77.

[65] Dick Field to Mrs. A.L. Field, December 26, 1943. Copy.

[66] Orfalea, *Messengers of the Lost Battalion*. pp.78-81 on Joerg and Graves.

[67] Ibid., pp. 88-91 on the Kinney Cameron training accident.

[68] Dick Field to Mrs. A.L. Field, February 17, 1943. Copy.

[69] Ibid.

[70] Ibid.

[71] Ibid.

[72] Ibid.

[73] Ibid.

[74] Ibid.

[75] Ibid.

[76] Undated envelope. Copy.

[77] Copy of this telegram and its envelope in possession of author.

[78] Dick Field to Mrs. R.J. Field, April 11, 1944. Copy.

[79] http://arcweb.sos.state.or.us/exhibits/ww2/services/induct.htm (accessed June 20, 2011).

[80] Orfalea, *Messengers of the Lost Battalion*, p.189.

[81] http://historichamptonroads.com/hm_patrick_henry.htm (accessed October 10, 2011). For a map of Camp Patrick Henry, see a web site dedicated to a soldier who passed through the camp, http://warren421.home.comcast.net/~warren421/welcome.html (accessed October 10, 2011).

[82] Orfalea, *Messengers of the Lost Battalion*, p. 113.

[83] For the size of the convoy, its departure date, and for the names of most of the ships in it, see http://tk-jk.net/stage3/Articles/Tuesdaynews6-20-06.html (accessed October 7, 2011). Orfalea states that all of the ships in the convoy, about "a hundred," were Liberty ships, but he does not mention Task Force 61 (ibid.).

[84] David M. Kennedy, *Freedom From Fear: The American People in Depression and War, 1929-1945* (New York, 1999), p. 649.

[85] On the ship assignments for the companies, see Orfalea, *Messengers of the Lost Battalion*, p. 113.

[86] On the number and custom of proposing names for Liberty ships, see http://www.usmm.org/libertyships.html (accessed October 7, 2011).

[87] See Kennedy, *Freedom From Fear*, pp. 649-650 and ibid. for the size and cargo capacity of a Liberty ship.

[88] http://www.usmm.org/libertyships.html (accessed October 7, 2011) for the speed at which the *Mulholland* could run.

[89] Orfalea, *Messengers of the Lost Battalion*, p. 113 on the length of the voyage and the food.

[90] Ibid., p. 114.

[91] http://tk-jk.net/stage3/Articles/Tuesdaynews6-20-06.html (accessed October 7, 2011).

[92] Ibid. details the attack. See also Orfalea, *Messengers of the Lost Battalion*, p. 115. One important contradiction between these two sources concerns the damage the convoy sustained. The web site article, written, recall, by a WW II Navy veteran who in all probability used official battle reports for his sources, states that no Allied ship sustained any damages. But Orfalea states fourteen ships were lost (p. 115).

[93] Rick Atkinson, *The Army at Dawn: The War in North Africa, 1942-1943* (New York, 2002), p. 69.

[94] Ibid., p. 87.

[95] Orfalea, *Messengers of the Lost Battalion*, p. 116.

[96] David M. Kennedy (editor), *The Library of Congress, World War II Companion* (New York, 2007), p. 313.

[97] Dick Field to Mrs. R.A. Field, May 24, 1945. Copy. Since the war in Europe ended earlier that month, this was the first uncensored letter Dick could write to his wife since his arrival in the ETO. He used the opportunity to send her a lengthy letter detailing where he had been in the ETO and some of what he had done.

[98] Orfalea, *Messengers of the Lost Battalion*, p. 116.

[99] Ibid.

[100] Ibid.

[101] Ibid., p. 118 for the date of the 551st arrival in Naples.

[102] http://www.volcanolive.com/vesusius.html (accessed October 25, 2011).

[103] Orfalea, *Messengers of the Lost Battalion*, pp. 119-121 for the train ride from Naples to Reggio de Calabria.

[104] Dick Field to Mrs. R.A. Field, May 24, 1945. Again, note that Dick made this observation in an uncensored letter.

[105] Orfalea, *Messengers of the Lost Battalion*, p. 121 on the stay of the 551st in Sicily.

[106] Dick Field to Ann, July 20, 1944. Copy.

[107] Dick Field to Ann, August 28, 1944. Copy.

[108] Dick Field to Mrs. R.J. Field, postmarked June 5, 1944. Copy.

[109] Dick Field to Ann, June 27, 1944. Copy.

[110] Dick Field to Ann, June 15, 1944. Copy.

[111] Dick Field to Ann, July 20, 1944. Copy.

[112] Orfalea, *Messengers of the Lost Battalion*, pp. 116-117.

[113] Ibid., p. 123.

[114] Dick Field to Ann, May 24, 1945.

[115] Dick Field to Ann, July 20, 1944.

[116] Ibid.

[117] Dick Field to Ann, May 24, 1945.

[118] Orfalea, *Messengers of the Lost Battalion*, p. 125

[119] Ibid., p. 126.

[120] Dick Field to Ann, July 20, 1944.

[121] Orfalea, *Messengers of the Lost Battalion*, p. 126.

[122] Samuel Eliot Morison, *The Invasion of France and Germany, 1944-1945* (New York, 1957; Edison, NJ, 2001 edition), pp. 221-222.

[123] Ibid., p. 221.

[124] Morison, *The Invasion of France and Germany*, p. 222.

[125] Ibid., p. 221.

[126] Alan F. Wilt, *The French Riviera Campaign of August 1944* (Carbondale, IL, 1981) p. 3.

[127] Dwight D. Eisenhower, *Crusade in Europe* (New York, 1948), pp. 282-283.

[128] William B. Breuer, *Operation Dragoon: The Allied Invasion of the South of France* (Novado, CA, 1987; 1996 edition), p. 20 for 2,500 year status of Marseilles as the primary port and for it population.

[129] For how Marseilles factored into the overall strategy, see Eisenhower, *Crusade*, pp. 281-283 and Morison, *The Invasion of France and Germany*, p. 226.

[130] Eisenhower, *Crusade*, p. 281.

[131] For the disagreement between Eisenhower and Churchill regarding Anvil, see Wilt, *The French Riviera Campaign*, pp. 2-3; Eisenhower, *Crusade*, pp. 281-284; Morison, *The Invasion of France and Germany*, pp. 222-223, 225-226, and 230-231.

[132] Wilt, *The French Riviera Campaign*, pp. 46-47. For Roosevelt's support of Anvil, see p. 58 and Morison, *The Invasion of France and Germany*, p. 222.

[133] Orfalea, *Messengers of the Lost Battalion*, p. 126 on Eisenhower's revival of Anvil.

[134] Wilt, *The French Riviera Campaign*, p. 56.

[135] Ibid., pp. 59-60 and Morison, *The Invasion of France and Germany*, p. 230.

---

[136] Captain Harry C. Butcher, USNR, *My Three Years with Eisenhower* (New York, 1946), p. 634.

[137] Orfalea, *Messengers of the Lost Battalion*, p. 40 on the training; p. 134 states that 826 men in the 551st left the Lido di Roma, and p. 134 also gives the time and date of departure from Lido di Roma as well as the destination. Breuer, *Operation Dragoon*, identifies the airfield as one hundred miles from Rome and also states that 842 men (796 enlisted and 46 officers) made up the 551st at that point in time (p. 189).

[138] Dick Field to Ann, May 24, 1945. See also, on the move to the airport, ibid., p. 130.

[139] Orfalea, *Messengers of the Lost Battalion*, p. 134.

[140] Ibid.

[141] Breuer, *Operation Dragoon*, p. 191 for the number of C-47s.

[142] Orfalea, *Messengers of the Lost Battalion*, p. 135.

[143] Dick has in his possession a copy of an undated letter Joe Killgore wrote sometime in the 1990s. The letter details Joe's recollections of August 15, 1944. Kilgore mentions how the troopers grease-painted their face. Michel de Trez, in *First Airborne Task Force: Pictorial History of the Allied Paratroopers in the Invasion of Southern France* (Belgium, 1998), p. 321 does the same.

[144] Ibid. The estimate of the weight a paratrooper carried is Dick's recollection.

[145] Orfalea, *Messengers of the Lost Battalion*, p. 141. Dick edited the list Orfalea quoted to also reflect his recollections.

[146] Ibid., p. 135.

[147] Wilt, *The French Riviera Campaign*, pp. 81-82 on the location of the invasion and weather conditions.

[148] Morison, *The Invasion of France and Germany*, p. 291.

[149] The numerical contribution of the various branches to Operation Dragoon is taken from Wilt, *The French Riviera Campaign*, pp. 64, 13, 87, 66 respectively and Morison, *The Invasion of France and Germany*, p. 237. Wilt cites nine thousand airborne troops (p. 90); Breuer, *Operation Dragoon*, p. 200 and Orfalea, *Messengers of the Lost Battalion*, p. 127 both use the ten-thousand-man statistic.

[150] Breuer, *Operation Dragoon*, p. 247.

[151] For the story of the Oran drop, see Atkinson, *The Army at Dawn*, pp. 87-91; for Sicily, see William B. Breuer, *Drop Zone Sicily, Allied Airborne Strike July 1943* (Novat, Ca., 1983).

[152] Breuer, *Operation Dragoon*, p. 38 identifies the mission of the FABTF and its code name, Rugby Force.

[153] Ibid., p. 39; also on Le Muy, Orfalea, *Messengers of the Lost Battalion*, p. 133.

[154] Breur, *Operation Dragoon*, p. 38 has a very detailed listing of the various airborne units that composed FABTF. See also Orfalea, *Messengers of the Lost Battalion*, p. 127 and Wilt, *The French Riviera Campaign*, p. 69. Rupert Graves, who had commanded the 551st in Georgia during the tragic training accident, was in charge of the 517th.

[155] de Trez, *First Airborne Task Force*, p. 8.

[156] Orfalea, *Messengers of the Lost Battalion*, p. 136. Orfalea identifies the number of 551st in the one-hundred-man pathfinder group as seventeen on p. 141.

[157] Ibid., p. 136.

[158] Ibid. Breuer, *Operation Dragoon*, p. 189 also identifies 6:00 P.M. as the drop time of the 551st.

[159] Breuer, *Operation Dragoon*, p. 129 gives 1,500-1,800 feet as the height at which the 551st exited the plane, with the customary height at 600-750 feet. Similarly, Orfalea, *Messengers of the Lost Battalion*, p. 144 quotes two members of the 551st as recalling 1,500-2,000 as the altitude; Orfalea gives 800-1,000 (p. 106) as the normal jump altitude. De Trez, *First Airborne Task Force*, p. 8 explains a higher drop height (he cites 1,500-1,800) due to the "high terrain in target areas."

[160] Killgore's letter from the 1990s identifies the order of the men at the door, waiting to jump.

[161] Killgore letter from the 1990s.

[162] Orfalea, *Messengers of the Lost Battalion*, p. 136 identifies LaMotte as the town.

[163] For the German defense erected against an airborne invasion, see ibid., p.145 and Breuer, *Operation Dragoon*, p. 25. Orfalea states that only two members of the 551st were "hooked" by Rommel's asparagus, although another one almost died from his injuries (p. 145).

[164] Orfalea, *Messengers of the Lost Battalion*, pp. 146-147 on the landing. There is a web site devoted to the history of the 551st— http://www.551stpib.com/newsite/history.html (accessed December 6, 2011). On the web site, casualties the battalion suffered in the ETO are listed by name in their respective companies. Dick found some errors in the listing for Company B, so the site should be used carefully.

[165] de Trez, *First Airborne Task Force*, p. 8 details the different jump times and DZs of the units that comprised Rugby Force.

[166] Orfalea, *Messengers of the Lost Battalion*, pp. 145-146 on the gliders and p. 146 on casualty figures for the FABTF's D-Day.

[167] Ibid., p. 146.

[168] Morison, T*he Invasion of France and Germany*, p. 249.

[169] Orfalea, *Messengers of the Lost Battalion*, p. 147.

[170] Morison, *The Invasion of France and Germany*, p. 249 on the capture of Le Muy and the number of POWs.

[171] Killgore letter from the 1990s.

[172] Dick Field e-mail to author, December 11, 2011.

[173] Orfalea, *Messengers of the Lost Battalion,* p. 133.

[174] Breuer, *Operation Dragoon*, p. 221.

[175] Ibid., p. 223; Orfalea, *Messengers of the Lost Battalion*, p. 151.

[176] Ibid, p. 152.

[177] Ibid. For the date when Draguignan fell, see also http://www.insigne.org/551-chronology.htm (accessed October 30, 2011).

[178] Orfalea, *Messengers of the Lost Battalion*, p. 156 on Draguignan casualties. Orfalea states that three men from the 551st were buried in the Draguignan

cemetery. Since two died on the 15th, in all likelihood they were buried in that cemetery. That would mean that one more died in the liberation of Draguignan.

[179] Dick Field to Ann, May 24, 1945. Copy.

[180] Orfalea, *Messengers of the Lost Battalion*, p. 157 on the one hundred degree temperatures and on the trip south.

[181] Ibid., p. 156. Orfalea covers the attack on Hill 105 (pp. 158-161) based upon recollections of men in the 551st.

[182] de Trez, *First Airborne Task Force*, p. 363 states that the battalion lost twenty-five men on Hill 105. Dick adds that "the majority were from Company B."

[183] Ibid. gives some history on the liberation of Cannes but uses D+10 as the date for when the 551st and the 509th moved toward Cannes. Orfalea, however, in *Messengers of the Lost Battalion*, p. 137, gives the date for Cannes' liberation as August 24th (D+9) as does Wilt, *The French Riviera Campaign*, p. 142. The August 24th date is used here.

[184] http://www.insigne.org/551-chronology.htm (accessed October 30, 2011). See also, map in Orfalea, *Messengers of the Lost Battalion*, p. 137 with dates of liberation.

[185] Dick Field to Esther Field, September 9, 1944. Copy.

[186] Orfalea, *Messengers of the Lost Battalion*, pp. 156, 167. For the campaign in southern France, Orfalea gives the final number of dead from the 551st as thirty and wounded as one hundred and fifty (p. 167).

[187] de Trez, *First Airborne Task Force*, p. 383 on the August 31st movement of the 551st to the area around La Turbie and its return to Nice.

[188] Morison, *The Invasion of France and Germany*, p. 291. A long ton is a British measurement of 2,240 pounds, whereas the American "short ton" is 2,000 pounds.

[189] For assessments on the success of Dragoon, see Wilt, *The French Riviera Campaign*, p. 166 and Breuer, *Operation Dragoon*, p. 249. For the weaknesses of German defenses in southern France, see Morison, *The Invasion of France and Germany*, p. 292. Morison explains the disadvantages German faced in defending the area--their "U-boats and Luftwaffe had been almost completely eliminated, available German surface craft were few and weak, the coastal batteries with few exceptions were poorly served, and the German ground forces, having no defense in depth, attempted no counterattack." Wilt, *The French Riviera Campaign* p. 76 notes that there was little chance that German forces in southern France could receive reinforcements. Wilt also explains that although "the German knew the approximate location and the exact date of the attack, there was little they could do about it" (p. 76).

[190] Breuer, *Operation Dragoon*, p. 247.

[191] Morison, *The Invasion of France and Germany*, p. 292.

[192] de Trez, *First Airborne Task Force*, p. 387.

[193] Orfalea, *Messengers of the Lost Battalion*, p. 169.

[194] On the truck journey from Nice to Villars-sur-Var, see de Trez, *First Airborne Task Force*, p. 387. On areas where they billeted, see Orfalea, *Messengers of the*

Lost Battalion, pp. 169-170 and de Trez, *First Airborne Task Force*, p. 387. Orfalea and de Trez identify St. Martin-Vesubie as the location of Company B.

[195] de Trez, *First Airborne Task Force*, p. 387 describes the higher altitude position of the Germans in respect to the Americans. He also summarizes the activities of the 551st in the period from September to mid-November.

[196] Orfalea, *Messengers of the Lost Battalion*, p. 189 and 180 respectively on the date its mission in the Maritime Alps ended and on the casualties it sustained.

[197] Ibid., p. 189.

[198] Ibid., pp. 189-190 for the trip south and their stay in Saint-Jeannet.

[199] Ibid., pp. 191-193.

[200] Ibid., p. 193.

[201] Ibid., pp.194-196 on Evans' pronouncement and on the orders received by Joerg. The quotation regarding the importance of the Battle of the Bulge, is from Charles MacDonald, *A Time for Trumpets: The Untold Story of the Battle of the Bulge* (New York, 1985; 2002 edition), p. 11.

[202] Orfalea, *Messengers of the Lost Battalion,* pp. 188-189. Most of the rounds were 150mm.

[203] MacDonald, *A Time for Trumpets*, pp. 11, 618.

[204] Eisenhower, *Crusade*, p. 353.

[205] On Hitler's goals, see Kennedy, *World War II Companion*, pp. 599-600 and Stanley Weintraub, *11 Days in December: Christmas at the Bulge, 1944* (New York, 2006), pp. 64, 12.

[206] On the importance of St. Vith and Bastogne, see Colonel R. Ernest Dupuy, *St. Vith, Lion in the Way: The 106th Infantry Division in World War II* (Washington, D.C., 1949), p. 2. Hugh M. Cole, *United States Army in World War II, The European Theater of Operations, The Ardennes: Battle of the Bulge* (Washington, D.C., 1965), p. 272 on St. Vith.

[207] Ibid., pp. 73, 305, 334.

[208] In the Battle of the Bulge, the 82nd Airborne Division consisted of the following units--the 504, 505, and 508 Parachute Infantry Regiments; the 325 Glider Infantry Regiment; the 376 and 456 Parachute FA [Field Artillery] Battalions; the 307 Airborne Engineer Battalion; and the 80 AAA [Anti-Aircraft Artillery] AW [Automatic Weapons] Battalion. MacDonald, *A Time for Trumpets*, p. 635.

[209] For information on the departure of the airborne divisions from the areas around Rheims for the Ardennes, see Cole, *United States Army*, p. 305 (he uses the phrase "motor march into Belgium") and Guy Lofaro, *The Sword of St. Michael, The 82nd Airborne Division in World War II* (Cambridge, MA, 2011), p. 434.

[210] Lofaro, *The Sword of St. Michael*, p. 441 quotes reports from the 504th and the 505th in detailing the trucks' journey.

[211] Cole, *United States Army*, p. 307 on Gavin's arrival and new orders; Lofaro, *The Sword of St. Michael*, pp. 439, 443 on new orders. Orfalea, *Messengers of the Lost Battalion*, p. 202 on location of Werbomont in respect to St. Vith; MacDonald, *A Time for Trumpets*, p. 433 on Gavin and Ridgway's HQs. Departure date from

Laon, and arrival date in Werbomont can be wound in Orfalea, *Messengers of the Lost Battalion*, pp. 196 and 202 respectively.

[212] Quotations in this paragraph are taken by Orfalea, *Messengers of the Lost Battalion*, pp. 220 and 209 respectively. The outlines of the Werbomont defense perimeter is from Lofaro, *The Sword of St. Michael*, p. 451; MacDonald, *A Time for Trumpets*, pp. 481, 445.

[213] Weintraub, *11 Days in December*, p. 22.

[214] Climatic conditions are taken from MacDonald, *A Time for Trumpets*, p. 28 and Cole, *United States Army*, p. 46.

[215] Orfalea, *Messengers of the Lost Battalion*, p. 226 and MacDonald, *A Time for Trumpets*, pp. 521-522.

[216] http://ancestry.com. U.S. World War II Army Enlistment Records, 1938-1946 (accessed January 3, 2012)..

[217] Lee Kennett, *G.I., The American Soldier in World War II* (New York, 1987; 1997 edition), p. viii.

[218] McManus, *The Deadly Brotherhood*, pp. 4, 7; Kennett, *G.I.*, pp. 128-129.

[219] Dick Field to Mrs. A.L. Field, December 26, 1943. Copy.

[220] Telephone conversation with Carol Field Folcarelli, September 12, 2010.

[221] http://www.presidency.ucsb.edu/ws/?pid=16485 (accessed January 2, 2012). Weintraub, *11 Days in December*, p. 144.

[222] Examples of Christmas meals are taken from Weintraub, *11 Days in December*, pp. 158, 152, 164, and 159 respectively.

[223] Orfalea, *Messengers of the Lost Battalion*, p. 232.

[224] Ibid., p. 235. For Gavin's reason for the raid, see p. 234.

[225] Ibid., pp. 241-242

[226] Ibid., p. 246.

[227] Nordyke, *All American*, p. 655.

[228] Orfalea, *Messengers of the Lost Battalion*, p. 250.

[229] Ibid., p. 234 on the location of the 551st in the week after Noirefontaine.

[230] Lofaro, *The Sword of St. Michael*, p. 483 on the general plan for the counteroffensive.

[231] The description of Gavin's plan is taken from Lofaro, *The Sword of St. Michael*, p.483; Orfalea, *Messengers of the Lost Battalion*, pp. 256-257, 300; and Nordyke, *All American*, p. 656.

[232] Orfalea, *Messengers of the Lost Battalion*, p. 257.

[233] Nordyke, *All American*, p. 655.

[234] The most detailed account of the movement of the 551st that first day of the counteroffensive, January 3, 1945, is found in Orfalea, *Messengers of the Lost Battalion*, pp. 257-271. The words "annihilation" and "slaughter" appear on p. 264. The 189 casualty-count is on p. 274.

[235] Ibid., p. 274 on Joerg's request.

[236] Specific details on the weather can be found in Nordyke, *All American*, p. 657; Lofaro, *Sword of St. Michael*, p. 484; and Orfalea, *Messengers of the Lost Battalion*, pp. 258, 260

[237] Orfalea, *Messengers of the Lost Battalion*, p. 272.
[238] Ibid., pp. 277-278.
[239] For the events of January 5th, see ibid., pp. 282-284.
[240] For the detachment and new attachment, see ibid., p. 292 and Nordyke, *All American*, p. 690.
[241] Orfalea, *Messengers of the Lost Battalion*, p. 294.
[242] Both quotations explaining why Rochelinval had to be taken are from ibid., pp. 294 and 293 respectively. The village's location one mile east of Dairomont is on p. 289.
[243] On battalion strength , see ibid., pp. 292, 299 and Nordyke, *All American*, p. 690. On German strength, see ibid., p. 295 and Nordyke, *All American*, p. 689.
[244] On the physical condition of the men, see Orfalea, *Messengers of the Lost Battalion*, p. 296.
[245] Ibid., p. 296.
[246] On the terrain and German defenses the 551st confronted, see ibid., pp. 295, 300 and Nordyke, *All American*, p. 691.
[247] Orfalea, *Messengers of the Lost Battalion*, pp. 327-329. After the war, the secretary of the 517th association blamed Joerg himself for outrunning artillery cover, although that is a questionable charge (p. 303).
[248] Ibid., pp. 297-298, 329.
[249] Ibid., p. 302.
[250] Nordyke, *All American*, p. 694.
[251] Ibid., pp. 692, 694. Orfalea, *Messengers of the Lost Battalion*, recounts the assault on pp. 305-312.
[252] Battalion strength and casualty numbers are taken from Orfalea, *Messengers of the Lost Battalion*, p. 321.
[253] Dick Field to Ann Field, May 24, 1945. Copy.
[254] Orfalea, *Messengers of the Lost Battalion*, p. 233.
[255] On the relief of the 82nd, and the trip to Juslenville, see ibid., p. 321.
[256] Ibid., p. 316 on Joerg and description of aid station as village schoolhouse.
[257] "Report of Physical Examination of Enlisted Personnel Prior to Discharge, Release from Active Duty or Retirement," date of examination December 26, 1945. Form WD AGO Form 38. This form is one filled out when Dick was discharged from the Army in Fort Dix, New Jersey. Copy.
[258] Dick Field to Ann Field, May 24, 1945. Copy.
[259] Information on Churchill Hospital and the 91st General Hospital is taken from http://med-dept.com/unit_histories/91_gen_hosp.php (accessed January 18, 2010).
[260] Geoffrey Perret, *There's A War To Be Won, The United States Army in World War* II (New York, 1991), pp. 434, 490-491.
[261] Orfalea, *Messengers of the Lost Battalion*, pp. 329-331 on the disbandment of the 551st.
[262] Ibid., p. 4.
[263] Dick Field to Ann Field, May 24, 1945. Copy.

[264] On the arrival of the 82nd at Suippes, the replacements, the division's three regiments, and the 509th, see Lofaro, *The Sword of St. Michael*, pp. 186, 525-526.
[265] Ibid., pp. 19, 554-555. Only one airborne division, the 11th, existed in the Pacific Theater.
[266] Dick wrote "Co. C" in the return address on his envelopes in letters to Ann and Esther. His placement in the 1st battalion is surmised from a reference in Lofaro, *The Sword of St. Michael*, p. 544 that details a friendly fire incident when the 505th crossed the Elbe. Dick vividly recalls that incident.
[267] On the Ruhr Pocket, see Orfalea, *Messengers of the Lost Battalion*, p. 338; Lofaro, *The Sword of St. Michael*, pp. 531-532; and Clay Blair, *Ridgway's Paratroopers, The American Airborne in World War II* (New York, 1985) pp. 566-568.
[268] On the arrival, duties, and living conditions of the 505th, see Lofaro, *The Sword of St. Michael*, pp. 531-533, 536-537.
[269] Ibid., p. 537 for the quotation and the new duties of the 82nd beginning April 15, 1945. Orfalea, *Messengers of the Lost Battalion*, p. 338 states that most German forces in the Ruhr Pocket surrender during April, with the final surrender on April 21st.
[270] Nordyke, *All American*, p. 742.
[271] Max Hastings, *Inferno, The World at War, 1939-1945* (New York, 2011), p. 592.
[272] Williamson Murray and Allan R. Millett, *A War to Be Won, Fighting the Second World War* (Cambridge, Massachusetts, 2000; 2001 printing), p. 480.
[273] Dick Field to Ann Field, May 24, 1945. Copy.
[274] On the trip from Cologne to Bleckede, and on the plan for the crossing, see Nordyke, *All American*, p. 744; Lofaro, *The Sword of St. Michael*, pp. 542-543; and Blair, *Ridgway's Paratroopers*, p. 583.
[275] Nordyke, *All American,* p. 745; Lofaro, *The Sword of St. Michael*, p. 543 for the landing plans.
[276] On the crossing, see Lofaro, *The Sword of St. Michael*, pp. 543-545; Dick Field to Ann Field, May 24, 1945, Copy; Blair, *Ridgway's Paratroopers*, p. 584.
[277] The intelligence officer is quoted in Lofaro, *The Sword of St. Michael*, p. 546. See also pp. 542 and 551 on the risk of the mission and casualty figures.
[278] Dick Field to Ann Field, May 24, 1945. Copy.
[279] Blair, *Ridgway's Paratroopers*, p. 590.
[280] Ibid., p. 569. Gavin was actually anxious to participate in the Pacific war now that the war in the ETO was over (Lofaro, *The Sword of St. Michael*, pp. 535-536.)
[281] Dick Field to Ann Field, May 6, 1945 and May 24, 1945. Copies.
[282] On the 82nd and its responsibilities for the POWs, see Lofaro, *The Sword of St. Michael*, p. 551 and Nordyke, *All American*, pp. 751, 757.
[283] Dick Field to Ann Field, May 6, 1945; Dick Field to Esther Field, May 6, 1945; Dick Field to Ann Field, May 24, 1945. Copies.
[284] Nordyke, *All American*, p. 761. Nordyke dates the 82nd move to Epinal as occurring on June 12th-15th. However, in a June 17th letter Dick wrote to Ann, he identifies Laon still as his location. Perhaps the 82nd moved to Epinal in stages.

285 Ibid., p. 762. See also Lofaro, *The Sword of St. Michael*, p. 556.
286 Nordyke, *All American*, p. 763.
287 Dick Field to Ann Field, August 17, 1945. Copy.
288 Ibid.
289 Ibid.
290 The point system is described in Lofaro, *The Sword of St. Michael*, p. 554. The demobilization process--the rate of discharge per month, the January 1946 information, and the quotations from Eisenhower--are taken from a January 22, 1946 issue of the *Daily Pacifican,* a newspaper published by the United States Army in the Pacific.
291 Nordyke, *All American*, p. 766 for details on the departure of the 82nd from Berlin and its arrival at Camp Chicago and then Camp Lucky Strike.
292 For information on the American camps around La Havre, especially Camp Lucky Strike, see Thomas Childers, *Soldiers from the War Returning: The Greatest Generation's Troubled Homecoming from World War II* (Boston, 2009), pp. 43, 110, 111-112. In addition, Childers gives more history on Camp Lucky Strike in another of his books, *In the Shadows of War: An American Pilot's Odyssey Through Occupied France and the Camps of Nazi Germany* (New York, 2002), p. 402. A very detailed web site on the camps is http://www.skylighters.org/special/cigcamps/cmplstrk.html (accessed September 25, 2011).
293 For details on the parade, see Lofaro, *The Sword of St. Michael*, p. 558.
294 On Levittowns, especially the one in Pennsylvania, see http://www.statemuseumpa.org/levittown.html (accessed January 30, 2012). For a web site created by past and present residents of Levittown, Pennsylvania, see http://www.levittowners.com (accessed January 30, 2012).
295 Orfalea, *Messengers of the Lost Battalion*, pp. 357-358.
296 Dan Morgan, *The Left Corner of My Heart, The Saga of the 551st Parachute Infantry Battalion* (Wauconda, WA, 1984), p. 4. For background to Morgan, both during and after the war, see Orfalea, *Messengers of the Lost Battalion*, pp. 84, 86, 98, 166, 334, 344, and 358.
297 Orfalea, *Messengers of the Lost Battalion*, pp. 358-359, 360; Morgan, *The Left Corner of My Heart*, unnumbered pages at the front of the book lists memorials and monuments.
298 On military honors conferred on the 551st, see Orfalea, *Messengers of the Lost Battalion*, pp. 331, 333 and Morgan, *The Left Corner of My Heart*, unnumbered pages at front of book.
299 On the historical slighting of the 551st, see Orfalea, *Messengers of the Lost Battalion*, pp. 331-334 and Morgan, *The Left Corner of My Heart*, pp. 439-440.